On
Religion

JOHN D. CAPUTO

On
Religion

London and New York

First published 2001
by Routledge
11 New Fetter Lane, London EC4P 4EE

Simultaneously published in the USA and Canada
by Routledge
29 West 35th Street, New York, NY 10001

Routledge is an imprint of the Taylor & Francis group

© 2001 John D. Caputo

Typeset in Joanna MT by
RefineCatch Limited, Bungay, Suffolk.
Printed and bound in Great Britain by
TJ International Ltd, Padstow, Cornwall.

British Library Cataloging in Publication Data
A catalogue record for this book is available from the British Library

Library of Congress Cataloging in Publication Data
Caputo, John D.
    On religion / John D. Caputo.
       p.   cm. – (Thinking in action)
    Includes bibliographical references.
    1. Religion—Philosophy.   I. Title.   II. Series
    BL51 .C325   2001
    200 – dc21   00–062807

ISBN 0 –415–23332–1 (hbk)
ISBN 0 –415–23333–X (pbk)

To Jacques Derrida,
who loosened my tongue

The Love of God
One

RELIGION IS FOR LOVERS

Any book entitled On Religion must begin by breaking the bad news to the reader that its subject matter does not exist. "Religion," in the singular, as just one thing, is nowhere to be found; it is too maddeningly polyvalent and too uncontainably diverse for us to fit it all under one roof. There are Western religions, Eastern religions, ancient religions, modern religions, monotheistic, polytheistic, and even slightly atheistic religions; too many to count, too many to master, in too many languages to learn. I am not complaining or making excuses. Indeed the uncontainable diversity of "religion" is itself a great religious truth and a marker of the uncontainability of what religion is all about. I am just trying to get started and I have to start somewhere. I am not trying to begin at the Absolute Beginning. I have no head for that. I am just trying to get something on the table.

By religion, therefore, let me stipulate, I mean something simple, open-ended, and old-fashioned, namely, the love of God. But the expression "love of God" needs some work. Of itself it tends to be a little vacuous and even slightly sanctimonious. To put it technically, it lacks teeth. So the question we need to ask ourselves is the one Augustine puts to himself in the Confessions, "what do I love when I love God?," or "what do I love when I love You, my God?," as he also put it, or,

1 **On** Religion

running these two Augustinian formulations together, "what do I love when I love my God?". Augustine, I should say at the start, will be my hero throughout these pages, although with a certain post-modern and sometimes unorthodox twist that might at times have provoked his episcopal wrath (he was a bishop, with a bishop's distaste for unorthodoxy).

I love this question in no small part because it assumes that anybody worth their salt loves God. If you do not love God, what good are you? You are too caught up in the meanness of self-love and self-gratification to be worth a tinker's damn. Your soul soars only with a spike in the Dow-Jones Industrial average; your heart leaps only at the prospect of a new tax break. The devil take you. He already has. Religion is for lovers, for men and women of passion, for real people with a passion for something other than taking profits, people who believe in something, who hope like mad in something, who love something with a love that surpasses understanding. Faith, hope, and love, and of these three the best is love, according to a famous apostle (I Cor. 13:13). But what do they love? What do I love when I love my God? That is their question. That is my question.

The opposite of a religious person is a loveless person. "Whoever does not love does not know God" (I John 4:8). Notice that I am not saying a "secular" person. That is because I am out to waylay the usual distinction between religious and secular in the name of what I shall call the "post-secular" or a "religion without religion." I include a lot of supposedly secular people in religion – this is one of my unorthodox tendencies that I hope to slip by the bishop's notice – even as I think a lot of supposedly religious people should look around for another line of work. A lot of supposedly secular people love something madly, while a lot of supposedly religious people love nothing more than getting their own way and bending others to their own will ("in the name of God"). Some people can be deeply and abidingly "religious" with or without theology, with or without the religions. Religion may be found with or without religion. That is my thesis.

Thus the real opposite of a religious person is a selfish and pusillanimous curmudgeon, a loveless lout who knows no higher pleasure than the contemplation of his own visage, a mediocre fellow who does not have the energy to love anything except his mutual funds. That is what the philosophers call an abusive definition, but I do not feel any great compunction about that, because the people I am abusing deserve it. They do not love God. What is worse than that? What can you say on their behalf? If you know, you should write your own book and defend them. This book is for those who love God, that is, for people who are worth their salt. The New Testament is peppered with references to salt (Matt. 5:13; Mark 9:50; Col. 4:6). Salt is my criterion of truth, and love is my criterion of salt.

But if my definition of irreligion, of the opposite of religion, is abusive, my definition of religion, the "love of God," sounds slightly smarmy and pietistic. The love of God is my north star, but it only provides me with a starting point, not a finish, a first word, not a last. Everything depends on the follow through, on facing up to this beautiful and provocative Augustinian question, "*what* do I love when I love my God?". Love is the measure. Every historical and social structure, everything created, generated, made, formed, or forged in time – and what is not? – should be measured against the love of God. Even religion – *especially* religion – insofar as religion takes historical and institutional form, must be tested to see how loyal it is to itself, to its religious vocation, which is the love of God. But the love of God *itself*, if ever we could find such a beautiful and precious jewel, is beyond criticism. Of the love of God *itself* I will hear no criticism; I will cup my ears.

Let us speak then of love. What does it mean to "*love*" something? If a man asks a woman (I am quite open to other permutations of this formula) "do you love me?" and if, after a long and awkward pause and considerable deliberation, she replies with wrinkled brow, "well, up to a certain point, under certain conditions, to a certain extent," then we can be sure that whatever it is she feels for this poor fellow it is not love and this relationship is not going to work out. For if love is the measure, the only measure of love is love without measure (Augustine again). One of the ideas behind "love" is that it represents a giving without holding back, an "unconditional" commitment, which marks love with a certain excess. Physicians counsel us to eat and exercise in measured moderation and not to overdo either. But there is no merit in loving moderately, up to a certain point, just so far, all the while watching out for number one (which is, alas, what we are often advised by a decadent "New Age" psychology). If a woman divorces a man because he turned out to be a failure in his profession and just did not measure up to the salary expectations she had for him when they married, if she complains that he did not live up to his end of the "bargain," well, that is not the sort of till-death-us-do-part, unconditional commitment that is built into marital love and the marital vow. Love is not a bargain, but unconditional giving; it is not an investment, but a commitment come what may. Lovers are people who exceed their duty, who look around for ways to do more than is required of them. If you love your job, you don't just do the minimum that is required; you do more. If you love your children, what would you not do for them? If a wife asks a husband to do her a favor, and he declines on the grounds that he is really not duty bound by the strict terms of the marriage contract to do it, that marriage is all over except for the paper work. Rather than rigorously defending their rights, lovers readily put themselves in the wrong and take the blame for the sake of preserving their love. Love, St. Paul said in his stunning hymn to love, is patient, kind, not puffed up or boastful; it bears all things, believes all things, hopes all things, endures all things (I Cor. 13). A world without love is a world governed by rigid contracts and inexorable duties, a world in which – God forbid! – the lawyers run everything. The mark of really loving someone or something is unconditionality and excess, engagement and commitment, fire and passion. Its opposite is a mediocre fellow, neither hot nor cold, moderate to the point of mediocrity. Not worth saving. No salt.

Then what about "God"? What about loving *God*? One of my main arguments in this essay is that "love" and "God" go together, for "God is love," as the New Testament tells us: "Beloved, let us love one another, because love is from God; everyone who loves is born of God and knows God. Whoever does not love does not know God, for God is love. . . . God is love and those who abide in love abide in God and God abides in them" (I John 4:7–8, 16). That is my Archimedean point, my true north. But notice how easily saying "God is love" slides over into saying "love is God." This slippage is provocative and it provides us with an exceedingly important and productive ambiguity, opening up a kind of endless substitutability and translatability between "love" and "God" that I shall also be exploring as we go along (and raising the eyebrow of a bishop or two along the way). As love is the first name of God, "of God" is also the best name we have for those who love. To love God is to love something deeply and unconditionally. But it is also true – there is no stopping this slippage or reversal – that to love deeply and unconditionally is to be born of God, to love God, for the name of God is the name of love, the name of what we love. That is why I will hear no criticism of this idea and why those who do not love God are loveless louts. That is also why the central and most pressing question is not whether I love God or whether there is a God to love, but "*what* do I love when I love my God?".

But where do we start – I am always trying to get started – if we want to get an idea of what we mean by "loving God"? An old and daunting problem, but my advice is as follows. When the Virgin Mary was told by the Angel Gabriel that she would conceive and bring forth a child, the first thing that Mary said, according to the gospel of Luke, was what any expectant virgin mother might be expected to say: "What are you talking about? I guarantee you, angel or not, that's impossible" (loosely translated). To which Gabriel responded, with characteristic archangelic composure, don't worry, "nothing will be impossible with God" (Luke 1:37). The second thing Mary said is what made her famous: "here I am," "fiat mihi secundum verbum tuum," in short, "yes, oui-oui" (in Franco-Aramaic). I will come back later on to the "yes," which I regard as an important and deeply religious notion and also closely linked to the idea of God, but for the moment I am interested in Luke's linking of "God" with "nothing is impossible." With God, all things are possible, very amazing things, even things that are, I am tempted to say, "unbelievable" (which are the things that most require belief), and even, God help us, "impossible" things. After Jesus told the story that it would be harder for the wealthy to enter the Kingdom of God than it would be for a camel to pass through the eye of a needle, he added, "For mortals it is impossible, but not for God; for God all things are possible" (Mark 10:27). So to get a start on the idea of loving God, let us take a closer look at what is for me, following Luke and Mark, a closely connected idea, "the impossible."

THE IMPOSSIBLE

To explain what I mean by "the impossible" I first need to explain what I mean by the "possible," and to explain the possible I need to talk about the "future," which is the domain of the possible. We say that we want the future to be "bright," "promising," "open." The force of the future is to prevent the present from closing in on us, from closing us up. The future pries open the present by promising us the possibility of something new, the chance of something different, something that will transform the present into something else. Let us make a distinction here. There is a relatively foreseeable future, the future for which we are planning, the future on which we are all hard at work, the future we are trying to provide for when we save for our retirement or when a corporate team sets up a long-term plan. Let us call that the "future present," by which I mean the future of the present, the future to which the present is tending, the momentum of the present into a future that we can more or less see coming. I have no intention of lightly dismissing this future. Institutional long-term plans, retirement plans, life insurance policies, plans for the future education of our children, all such things are very serious, and it is foolish and irresponsible to proceed without them. But there is another future, another thought of the future, a relation to another future, which is the future that is unforeseeable, that will take us by surprise, that will come like a thief in the night (I Thess. 5:2) and shatter the comfortable horizons of expectation that surround the present. Let us call this the "absolute future." When it comes to the relative future, the future present, we have "reasonable expectations," "cautious optimism," "bulls and bears," but as regards the absolute future we must be like the lilies of the field who sow not, nor do they reap, but who are willing to go with what God provides, which also means that they are ready for anything. For the relative future we need a good mind, a decent computer, and horse sense, those three; for the absolute future, we need hope, faith, and love, these three.

With the "absolute" future we are pushed to the limits of the possible, fully extended, at our wits' end, having run up against something that is beyond us, beyond our powers and potentialities, beyond our powers of disposition, pushed to the point where only the great passions of faith and love and hope will see us through. With the "absolute future," I maintain, we set foot for the first time on the shore of the "religious," we enter the sphere of religious passion, and we hit upon a distinctively "religious category." Let me clarify this. By the "religious" I do not mean some preternatural event in a Stephen King novel, or even an extraordinary visitation by a supernatural being like an angel. Of course, that is exactly what Luke's story of the Annunciation to Mary was, but that is a function of great religious narratives, in which we find human experience writ large, the defining features of our life magnified in moving and unforgettable stories, in brilliant religious figures. But having a religious sense of life is a very basic structure of our lives – it is not like worrying about being abducted by an alien – that should be placed alongside other very basic things, like having an artistic sense or political sense, experiences that belong to anyone who is worth their salt (more salt). The religious sense of life is tied up with having a future, which is something we *all* have, and the "absolute future" is a basic part of having a future. So instead of distinguishing "religious people," the ones who go to church on Sunday morning, from non-religious people, the ones who stay home and read *The Sunday New York Times*, I would rather speak of the religious *in* people, in all of us. I take "religion" to mean the being-religious of human beings, which I put on a par with being political or being artistic. By "the religious," I mean a basic structure of human experience and even, as I hope to show, the very thing that most constitutes human experience as experience, as something that is really happening. I do not confine religion to something confessional or sectarian, like being a Muslim or a Hindu, a Catholic or a Protestant, although I hasten to add that the great religions of the world are important and without them we would quickly lose sight of religious categories and practices, which means that we would lose something basic. And once again, we need to remind ourselves, the religious sense of life would never mean just one thing for everybody, as if it had some sort of common ahistorical, universal, transcendental structure. I try to swear off thinking like that about anything.

With a notion like the absolute future, we move, or we are moved, past the circle of the present and of the foreseeable future, past the manageable prospects of the present, beyond the sphere in which we have some mastery, beyond the domain of sensible possibilities that we can get our hands on, into a darker and more uncertain and unforeseeable region, into the domain of "God knows what" (literally!). Here we can at best feel our way, like a blind man with a stick, unsure and unsteady, trying to be prepared for something that will take us by surprise, which means trying to prepare for something for which we cannot be prepared. We cross over the border of rational planning methods, venturing into the sort of thing that makes corporate managers nervous, venturing out onto *terra incognita*. The absolute future is not much help in planning an investment strategy, where the idea is to guess the trends; nonetheless, as every fund manager eventually finds out, it belongs irreducibly to the structure of life in time. This is the sphere of the impossible, of something of whose possibility we just cannot conceive. But of course the impossible happens, which is the import of the story of the Annunciation to the Virgin Mary. So it is not simply or absolutely impossible, like "*p* and *not-p*," which would reduce it to incoherence, but what the French philosopher Jacques Derrida calls "*the* impossible," meaning something whose possibility we did not and could not foresee, something that eye has not seen, nor ear heard, that has never entered into the mind of human beings (I Cor. 2:9). So I am plainly advising us to revisit the idea of the impossible and to see our way clear to thinking the possibility of the impossible, of *the* impossible, of the possible as the "im-possible," and to think of God as the "becoming possible of the impossible," as Derrida also says.

The impossible is a defining religious category – and this is a central motif of this study – the stuff of which religion is made. When the Latin comic poet Terence wrote that since what we wish for is impossible, we would have more peace if we sought only the possible, he was advising us to give up religion. For with God, as Gabriel told a very surprised virgin, everything is possible, even *the* impossible. That is what we mean by God. The impossible, if I may be so bold, is all part of a divine day's work for God, part of God's job description. Of course, a virginal conception is not all part of a day's work for the rest of us, but the Scriptures are instructing us about the miraculousness of life, about those unforeseeable events, large or small, that elicit an "it's a miracle!" from us. The name of God is the name of the chance for something absolutely new, for a new birth, for the expectation, the hope, the hope against hope (Rom. 4:18) in a transforming future. Without it we are left without hope and are absorbed by rational management techniques. But that chance is not without risk, because we never know who is going to come knocking at our door; it could be Gabriel himself or it could be a devil. With the absolute future there are no absolute guarantees, no contracts or warranties. With the absolute future, there is a lot of risk, so faith, hope, and love have to work around the clock.

The impossible, I said, is what makes experience to be *experience*, makes it truly worthy of the name "experience," an occasion in which something really "happens," as opposed to the regular grooves and tick-tock time of humdrum life, when nothing much is really going on. The impossible is what gives life its salt. But notice that if the impossible is the condition of any real experience, of experience itself, and if the impossible is a defining religious category, then it follows that experience itself, all experience, has a religious character, whether or not you march yourself off to church on Sunday morning now that your mother is no longer there to get you out of bed. That religious edge to experience, that notion of life at the limit of the possible, on the verge of the impossible, constitutes a religious structure, the religious side of every one of us, with or without bishops or rabbis or mullahs. That is what I mean by "religion without religion" (to borrow another phrase from Derrida), the main idea I shall be defending throughout these pages.

The present and the future-present fall under the range of our powers, our potencies, our possibilities. Here things are manageable, cut to size and proportioned to our knowledge, so that we know what to do in the present situation and what to expect in the future. Here we are self-possessed and we have our bearings. This is the sphere of what the medieval theologians called the "cardinal" virtues, the four strictly philosophical virtues of "prudence, justice, fortitude, and temperance," upon which human life is propped as upon the four hinges (*cardines*) of a table. These are the virtues of the self-possessed, of the best and the brightest, what Aristotle called the "*phronimoi,*" the men (and he meant *men*) of practical wisdom, of insight and practical know-how, the well-hinged who know what is what, the men of means who went to all the best schools and who set the pace for the rest of us who are lower down on Aristotle's very aristocratic list. But when we come unhinged, when our powers and our potencies are driven to their limits, when we are overwhelmed, exposed to something we cannot manage or foresee, then, in that limit situation of the possibility of the impossible, we experience the limits, the impossibility, of our own possibilities. Then we sink to our knees in faith and hope and love, praying and weeping like mad. These are what the theologians call (somewhat chauvinistically) the "theological" virtues, by which they mean that we have come up against the impossible. Here, in the sphere of these limit situations, we are asked to believe what seems incredible (remember Mary, or father Abraham trekking his way to Moriah). For after all, to believe what seems highly credible or even likely requires a minimum of faith, whereas to believe what seems unbelievable, what it seems impossible to believe, that is really faith. If you have real faith, Jesus said, you could say to the mountain, "'move from here to there,' and it will move; and nothing will be impossible for you" (Matt. 17:20). So, too, to hope when all seems hopeless, to "hope against hope," as St. Paul says (Rom. 4:18), that is really hope, as opposed to the sanguinity that comes when the odds are on our side, which is the hope of a mediocre fellow. Finally, to dare to love someone far above our station, like a beggar in love with a princess, or to dare to think that someone so wonderful could love us, to dare to love in such an impossible situation, that is love worth its salt. Or, to go to a further and still more paradoxical extreme: to love someone who is not lovable. It is no great feat, after all, to love the loveable, to love our friends and those who tell us we are wonderful; but to love the unlovable, to love those who do not love us, to love our enemies – that is love. That is impossible, the impossible, which is why we love it all the more. So the unhinged life of love and hope and faith is saltier and more passionate and more worth living than that of Aristotle's well-hinged *phronimoi* who swing back and forth effortlessly and make it all look easy (even if it takes a lot of training).

Religion, I say at the risk of being misquoted, is for the unhinged. (That is, for lovers.) In religion, the time, time itself, is always out of joint. The religious sense of life awakens when we lose our bearings and let go, when we find ourselves brought up against something that exceeds our powers, that overpowers us and knocks us off our hinges, something impossible vis-à-vis our limited potencies. The religious sense of life kicks in when we are solicited by the voices of the impossible, by the possibility of the impossible, provoked by an unforeseeable and absolute future. Here is a realm where things do not bend to our knowledge or our will and we are not calling the shots. We are out of our element. This is God's element, not ours, the element of the impossible, God's realm or "Kingdom," where God rules. Something, I know not what, some element in things exceeds our grasp and eludes our reach. Here things are astir with some element of chance beyond our best-laid plans, some future that we cannot see, something that by withdrawing from sight nonetheless draws us out of ourselves and draws us on, something for which we pray and weep. Our sense of reality and of its limits is disturbed; our sense of what is possible and impossible begins to tremble, to destabilize, to become unsteady and uncertain. We begin to lose our grip and find ourselves in the grip of something that carries us along. We are exposed, vulnerable, expectant, in motion, moving, being moved, by the impossible. We are transformed.

Our only recourse is to hang on by our teeth, that is, to have faith and hope, and to love this possibility of an impossible and unmasterable future which is not in our hands. Love and hope and faith are the virtues of the impossible, taking the measure of the immeasurable future. The borders of the possible are safe but flat, sure but narrow, well defined but confining, and they stake out the lines of an unsalted and mediocre life, without a passionate hope, where nothing *really* happens and all present systems will do just fine. If at the end of our lives we find that all our hopes have been sensible and moderate and measured by the horizon of the future present, if we have never been astir with the impossible, then we shall also find that on the whole life has passed us by. If safe is what you want, forget religion and find yourself a conservative investment counselor. The religious sense of life has to do with exposing oneself to the radical uncertainty and the open-endedness of life, with what we are calling the absolute future, which is meaning-giving, salt-giving, risk-taking. The absolute future is a risky business, which is why faith, hope, and love have to kick in. Our hearts are restless (*"inquietum est cor nostrum"*), Augustine said, astir with the possibility of renewal and rebirth, pregnant with an absolute future, an absolute surprise, just like the Virgin Mary.

Religion on my telling is a pact or "covenant" with the impossible. To have a religious sense of life is to long with a restless heart for a reality beyond reality, to tremble with the possibility of the impossible. If the religious sense of life is sometimes thought of in terms of eternity, under the influence of Plato, my advice is to rethink it in terms of time, as a temporal way to be, a way to ride the waves of time, trying to catch its swells while trying not to end up like a drowned rat. That is why religious narratives are filled with so many miracle stories, which are stories of transforming change more stunning than anything Lewis Carroll dared imagine could happen to Alice – virgins becoming mothers, mountains moving on command, seas parting, the dead rising from the grave, and – most importantly, because this is what these stories are all about – sinners being forgiven and given a new heart, *metanoia*. To forgive is to lift the weight of the past and give someone a new lease on life, a new future, which is arguably the most basic thing Jesus had to say.

The Scriptures are filled with narratives in which the power of the present is broken and the full length and breadth of the real open up like a flower, unfolding the power of the possible, the power of the impossible beyond the possible, of the hyper-real beyond the real. So rather than being carried off to some illusory and fantastic realm, which is what critics of religion like Freud and Marx have concluded, faith, hope, and love are what we need to keep up with what is really going on in the real beyond the real, the open-ended hyper-real beyond the constricting limits of the present. Rather than hallucinations, faith, hope, and love are what we need to have a real and transforming experience. "When you send forth your spirit, they are created; and you renew the face of the earth," the psalmist sings (Ps. 104: 30). Embedded in the biblical idea of God as creator is the idea of re-creation. God cannot simply spend six days creating the world and then throw the tools on the truck and drive off for a long weekend. We require God to be on the job around the clock, for part of the job of making all things in the first place is to make all things *new*, again and again. We are not content to be born, but we want to be born anew, born again, as the Bible-thumpers like to sing and shout (and I am thumping right along with them on that!). Every "yes" – remember Mary's "yes" – naturally solicits a second "yes," a confirmation and prolongation of the first "yes," which insures that we do not go back on our word. The structure of the "yes," which goes to the heart of human experience, is a structure of doubling or repetition, of "yes, yes," which is pretty much what the Hebrew "Amen" means – *oui, oui*, so be it, three cheers, right on! Yes, yes to what is coming, to the God of yes, to the becoming possible of the impossible.

This also explains why religion has a *prophetic* dimension. But by "prophetic" I do not mean perfecting our predictive powers about the future-present, foreseeing what the future holds – as if being religious were something like being a weatherman. I am referring to what is called in the Jewish and Christian traditions "messianic" hope and expectation, which looks forward to the peace and justice of the messianic age. Even Karl Marx, who fancied himself a cold-hearted scientist who was dispassionately exposing the futility of religious illusion in the name of revolutionary historical progress, had a bit of the wild-eyed Jewish prophet about him. As anyone who knows anything about prophetic religion can see, Marx's "science" of political economy, which purported to have calculated the cold economic laws that turn the wheels of history (the side of Marx that turned out to be a howler), was a transcription of a prophetic passion, of a prophetic longing for the messianic age (while he thought he was debunking religion). Marx was praying and weeping for an age in which the rich stop feeding off the poor and making their fortunes off the bent backs of the most defenseless people in our society, off minorities and immigrants, women and children. That is the best side of Marx, the most enduring side, his prophetico-religious side, the way that even he continued to say a little prayer at night to the Hebrew Lord of history, just before nodding off (even if he did not remember a thing about it in the morning). That is a Marxism to which anyone who is not a loveless lout should say "yes, yes," should devoutly pray "come," "may Thy Kingdom come." Marx is descended from a long line of Jewish prophets, which is why, to the horror of Pope John Paul II – who divides the laurels with Ronald Reagan as the World Historical Conqueror of the Evil Empire – certain versions of Marx's atheism play so well in the churches of the poor. That is also why I think the distinction between theism and atheism is a little more unstable than people think, including most popes and bishops.

THE SECRET

I am all along building up the nerve to pose my question, to really *ask* my guiding question, which I have learned from St. Augustine, "what do I love when I love my God?". Everything depends on this question. It is my un-cardinal question – which is, no doubt, why it can make bishops nervous – the question of the unhinged. But before taking it up directly, I must first, once again following St. Augustine, make a confession. This confession comes accompanied by a recommendation that we all join in, because I have no intention of being left all alone twisting slowly in the wind of this confession while everyone else comes off looking innocent as a lamb. I am no phallic hero of the solitary leap and I have no heart for a lonely plunge into the abyss. I confess that I am unhinged, that I do not know who I am. But I highly recommend that we all hold hands and make a common confession that we are all unhinged and do not know who we are. We all want to know who we are and what our lives are "about" – that is our first, last, and constant concern. That is the passion of our lives, and it is a deeply religious passion. For better or worse (it depends on which day you ask me), we do not simply live but we wonder why; for better or worse, we do not simply live but we dream of things that never have been and wonder why not (Edward "Teddy" Kennedy's beautiful eulogy of Robert "Bobby" Kennedy). We are not content with life, with the limits that the present and the possible press upon us, but we strive and strain for something or other, we know not what. My modest contribution to that ageless restlessness of the human heart, the one small thing I hope to add to the *philosophia perennis*, is this: We do not know who we are – *that* is who we are. "*Quaestio mihi factus sum*" (it sounds better in Latin) is the way Augustine put it: "I have been made a question unto myself," echoing St. Paul (Rom. 7:15). Who am I? I am one who finds his life a question, whose life is always being put in question, which is what gives life its salt. We seek but do not find, not quite, not if we are honest, which does not discourage the religious heart but drives it on and heightens the passion, for this is one more encounter with the impossible. We may and we must have our opinions on the subject; we must finally reach a judgment and take a stand about life, but my advice is to attach a coefficient of uncertainty to what we say, for even after we have taken a stand, we still do not know who we are. We do not Know The Secret (notice the caps!).

Let there be no misunderstanding: I am not recommending a life of ignorance or of fence-sitting, of the comfort of finding the spot that precedes the "either/or," the fictitious peace of a space that somehow eludes the pull of competing forces, without siding or deciding one way or the other. Far from it; I have defined life in terms of salt and passion, religious passion, a passion for the impossible. But I am saying that the condition of this passion is non-knowing, that non-knowing is the inescapable element in which decisions are reached, which intensifies their passion. This non-knowing is not a simple garden-variety ignorance but rather more like what the mystics call a *docta ignorantia*, a learned or wise ignorance, that knows that we do not know and knows that this non-knowing is the inescapable horizon in which we must act, with all due decisiveness, with all the urgency that life demands. For life does not take a break, it does not let up its demands on us for a hour or two while we all break for lunch and a bit of a nap. We are required to act, but our decisions are covered by a thin film, a quiet and uneasy sense, of unknowing.

I am not trying to be discouraging. Far from it. I do not regard "the secret" to be all bad news but part of an upbeat and salutary minimalism that proceeds on the assumption that we get the best results by confessing fully the difficulty of the human condition and not putting too high a spin on things or too good a face on our predicament. The secret, on my hypothesis, is that there is no Secret. I am not saying all this in the service of a kind of hip academic skepticism, of a phallic, modish nihilism that is one of the luxuries of life in the tenured lane. On the contrary – to put it in terms that every investor in mutual funds will understand – I think that in the long run this pays the best returns, even if in the short run it is unnerving. As far as I can tell, and I think that this is essential to the unhinging and impassioning sense of life that I am trying to describe, we are not hard wired to some Transcendental Super-Force which communicates to us The Secret about The Meaning of our lives, or of the universe, or of good and evil, on the condition that we pray and fast and have no impure thoughts. That, I think, is how a lot of people think about religion, including a lot of religious people themselves, and I am trying to talk them out of it. As a rule of thumb, I should add, the best way to flag the tendency that I am cautioning against is to capitalize it [It]. We have not, to my knowledge, been visited by some Super-Revelation, some Apocalyptic Unveiling, that settles all our questions. Nor have we, I should add, come up with some Super-Method in philosophy or even in science that will, so long as we follow It (The Method) rigorously, expose the Essence or Hyper-essence of Reality, that will steer us through the stormy waves of becoming or cut through the veil of appearances. We cannot, by science, philosophy, or religion, situate ourselves safely in some privileged spot above the mortal fray below having gained the high ground of a Privileged Access to the Way Things Are, which distinguishes "us" (philosophers, physicists, true believers, etc.) from the poor beggars down there in quotidian life who wander about two headed and do not know The Way. We all need a "way," I am not denying that, but I deny that anyone has the authority to Capitalize their way. There is no way to know The Way, no way that I know, anyway.

By confessing up front that we do not know who we are, that we are cut off from The Secret, we find ourselves forced constantly to traffic in "interpretations," the inescapability of which is a good way to define "hermeneutics," a word that has had some currency among contemporary academics. I do not recommend ignorance and I am not saying that there is no truth, but I am arguing that the best way to think about truth is to call it the best interpretation that anybody has come up with yet while conceding that no one knows what is coming next. There are lots of competing truths battling with one another for their place in the sun, and the truth is that we have to learn to cope with the conflict. The skies do not open up and drop The Truth into our laps. Pressing this hermeneutic point about the inescapability of interpretation will also force a shift in what we mean by "truth," a shift into doing the truth, which will be a little like doing the impossible. I shall take this up in the fifth chapter, where I shall argue that this is especially characteristic of what we mean by "religious truth." For by a "religion without religion" I do not mean a religion without truth.

We are bereft, alas, of any apocalypse that unveils The Secret to us. We all pull on our pants one leg at a time and do our best to make it through the day. The secret is that there is no Secret, no capitalized Know-it-all Breakthrough Principle or Revelation that lays things out the way they Really Are and thereby lays to rest the conflict of interpretations. When we open our mouths, it is only we who are speaking, we poor existing individuals, as Kierkegaard liked to put it, and we would be ill advised to think that we are the Mouthpiece of Being or the Good or of the Almighty. But on my hypothesis, that is not bad news, because it tends to check the spread of people who confuse themselves with Being, or the Good, or the Almighty, who think that they have been sent into the world to tell the rest of us what God or Being or Nature (or Whatever) thinks, when in fact what we are hearing is nothing more than the views of Harry Gutentag, who is a decent enough chap if you get to know him but who tends to take himself a little too seriously.

Nor am I denying what we call the "Holy Scriptures" or the "Word of God." I am just trying to come up with a good description of what that means by trying to situate it within the element of unknowing, within this psalm to learned ignorance whose harp I am plucking at the moment. Hence I will continue to stick to my minimalist hypothesis even if we include a Book of Apocalypse, or of Revelation, in our sacred Scriptures. For we lack an apocalyptic revelation that this Book is "The Apocalypse," which is something that the believers in that Book take on faith, which means through a glass darkly, which means *sans* apocalypse. Even the Apocalypse is *sans* apocalypse. That means that the believers in that Book should temper their claims about The Revelation they (believe they) have received, since it is their interpretation that they have received a revelation, while not everyone else agrees. A revelation is an interpretation that the believers believe is a revelation, which means that it is one more competing entry in the conflict of interpretations. Believers should accordingly resist becoming triumphalistic about what they believe, either personally or in their particular community. Apart from the intrinsic merits of the book about whose interpretation we can all argue (and argue and argue), what they mainly have to offer in support of their belief that this is The Revelation is the fact that they believe it, or that it has been believed for centuries (one reason for which, history frequently teaches us, is the fate that was visited upon those who declined to believe it). They do not establish anything except their own mean-spiritedness by calling everyone else "infidels" or by looking down on everyone else whom they accuse of lacking "transcendence" in their lives. To be sure, as I am also arguing, religion does not have a corner on the market of pretending to Know The Secret. I would recommend the same modesty to scientists and philosophers, who should likewise resist adopting apocalyptic and capitalizing attitudes toward Physics or Metaphysics, lest these two otherwise modest and respectable enterprises, together or separately, succumb to the illusion that it is they who have seized the soft underbelly of Nature, or Being, or Reality, that they, if I may say so, have their finger on Being's button.

Confessing that we have no access to The Secret introduces a salutary caution into our lives which tends to contain the violence, the intellectual "road rage," that threatens to break out whenever we run up against something "different." The different is the *bête noire* of the faithful. But the effects of this confession are not only critical and negative, but highly affirmative and closely connected to the religious passion for the impossible that I am trying to describe. For if the secret is that there is no Secret, then it follows that we can only and indeed must believe, and indeed that we must believe *something*. When I say that we do not know who we are, I do not have my chin on my chest. I am not recommending despondency and despair and that we give up the search. Like everybody else, I would like to know as much as I can about as many things as possible and I have spent a small fortune on my library. I am not composing my "lamentations," not letting out a haunting wail that everything is vanity, a useless Sisyphean labor. On the contrary, this is all part of an upbeat and affirmative operation that recognizes that we are called upon to invent and reinvent ourselves or – since I am talking about the sort of thing over which we do not have mastery – to let ourselves be reinvented, to let ourselves be overtaken by the impossible. I am asking that we open ourselves toward a future we cannot see coming, whose coming we can see only darkly and in a mirror, for which nonetheless we passionately *hope and long*. Rather than a Sisyphean lament I prefer a great and giant "yes" like the titillating "yes" that Molly Bloom delivers at the end of *Ulysses*. "And yes, I said yes, I will, Yes." Very rousing, very arousing. If ever I broke my own rule, "yes" ("Yes") would be the only thing I would allow myself to capitalize: yes to the future, to what is coming, to possibilities that eye has not seen or ear heard, to the possibility of the impossible, yes to the God of yes, to *"Ja"*-weh. *Oui, oui*, amen. Yes, God is yes. Yes, yes to my God.

Now at long last I have gained the heart to take up our question and to return to my dear St. Augustine, whom we find praying and weeping over himself back in the *Confessions*, in scenes so intimate that we blush to witness them, in words so private that we are embarrassed to overhear them.

WHAT DO I LOVE WHEN I LOVE MY GOD?

Augustine's opening line in the *Confessions* is that our hearts are restless and will not rest until they rest in God, which I have transcribed a little impudently by saying that we are all a little unhinged. We are driven hither and yon by one desire after another and sometimes by several desires at once, and we shall get no peace until we rest in "God," for the name of God is the name of what we love and desire. Whatever that may be. Then the real question shifts to the one that we have been following: *what* do I love when I love you, my God? You know that I love you, O Lord, Augustine says to God. You know,

Lord, and I know as well, that I am after something, driven to and fro by my restless search for something, by a deep desire, indeed by a desire beyond desire, beyond particular desires for particular things, by a desire for I-know-not-what, for something impossible. Still, even if we are lifted on the wings of such a love, the question remains, *what* do I love, *what* am I seeking? When Augustine talks like this, we ought not to think of him as stricken by a great hole or lack or emptiness which he is seeking to fill up, but as someone overflowing with love who is seeking to know where to direct his love. He is not out to see what he can get, but out to see what he can give.

What is the name of what I love when I love my God? Since we are told that God is love, this question, I have said, tends to draw us into a circle that makes bishops everywhere nervous. Is it the case, as Augustine the bishop thought, that whenever we are carried away by the love of something, anything at all, it is really God whom we are seeking, but we simply have not come to realize that it is God whom we love, rather the way I see Peter coming even if I do not know it is Peter? Or might it be the other way around, that the name of God is a name we confer on things we love very dearly, like peace or justice or the messianic age? Which one is the example of which? Is love a way of exemplifying *God*? Or is God a name we have for exemplifying *love*? Which is which? What is what?

Given what I have been saying about the Secret, I must insist on the productivity and fertility of keeping that question open. If, in the orthodox view of the councils of the confessional faiths, love is one of the predicates or names we give to God, and God is decidedly the subject, then I am trying to leave a little space for heterodoxy. Bishops and cardinals are "hingers" who try to hang religion on the Right

Teaching, so that the doors of orthodoxy will swing smoothly open for the believers and tightly shut to the infidels, while I am inclined to think that we have all been unhinged by the secret, and that this is what gives life salt and genuine religious passion. I am interested in drawing the lines, not between the orthodox and the heterodox, or even between theists and atheists, or religious and secular. My cardinal distinction is between the salty and the saltless, which is how I mark off the different ways of loving God, with whom nothing is impossible, which is the defining mark of religious passion. Augustine says that God is love and that what we love when we love our God is God, and that when "non-believers" (himself included, before his conversion) go off in search of other things, whether it be very sublime things like justice or very low-down things like satisfying lust or greed, they are really engaged in a more or less enlightened or benighted search for God, except they do not realize that it is God for whom they search.

But, in my opinion, however tightly Augustine tried to close this door, he left it slightly ajar. For Augustine's question allows us to see that the passion for God has a wider sweep than this, and his question continues to stir even after Augustine thinks he has settled it. That is, I would keep Augustine's question open, give it a full throttle *as a question*, and treat it as a crucial and permanent part of the passion of our lives, of the *quaestio mihi factus sum* of which he spoke. When we put our head down and love God with all our strength, we do not know whether love is an exemplification of God or God is an exemplification of love. Or whether justice is one of the names we use to speak about God or whether the name of God is a way we have of speaking about justice. Or the impossible (the list goes on). We confess that we remain confused about this point and that we do not know how to resolve the confusion.

Augustine's question – "what do I love when I love my God?" – persists as a life-long and irreducible question, a first, last, and constant question, which permanently pursues us down the corridors of ours days and nights, giving salt and fire to our lives. That is because that question is entangled with the other persistent Augustinian question, "*who am I?*", to which, as we have seen above, Augustine replies in the powerful tenth book of the *Confessions* "a soil of difficulty and of great sweat." In your eyes, O Lord, he says, "I have become a question to myself." So these two questions, the question of God and the question of the self, go hand in hand for Augustine. So much God, so much self: the more I am inwardly tossed about by what I love, the more I am tossed about by the question of who I am, in virtue of which this sense of being a "self" is stirred up and intensified. That is why I think that I am being very Augustinian when I say: we do not know who we are – *that* is who we are. I do not question the self, but I treat the self as a question. When we confess that we do not know what we love when we love our God, we are also confessing that we do not know who we are, we who love our God. Who am I?, I ask with Augustine, and the answer is, I am a question unto myself. Who am I? The answer that comes back is another question; the answer is to keep questioning, to keep the question alive – that is what a "self" is – to keep questioning and to love God, to love God and to do what you will (which is still another interesting thing Augustine said, although I am giving it a spin). What do I love when I love my God? Is it God? Is it justice? Is it love itself? Once again, the answer is another question. I am the one who troubles himself about this, and the name of God is the name of what I am troubling myself about. I am being turned and tossed about (*perturbatio*) by the impossible.

Conservative, orthodox, and right-wing religious types will think that I am waffling, that I am trying to dodge the question and avoid giving an answer. Actually, the opposite is true. My idea is to give the passion of this question full throttle. My whole idea is that, since I doubt that there is something called "The Answer" to this question, in caps, the only thing we can do is to *answer*. The way Mary answered "here I am" when Gabriel broke the amazing news to the Virgin about the birth of a son, or the way Abraham answered "here I am" when the Lord demanded the death of his son (a very problematic story that needs a careful gloss). The whole idea is to *respond*, to *do* the truth, to make truth happen, *facere veritatem*, as Augustine said, to do justice, to do the impossible, to make the mountain move, to go where I cannot go, even if I do not know who I am or what I love when I love my God. My "responsibility" is not just to speculate at my word processor about the name of God but to *do* justice. When the love of God calls, we had better answer. When the demand for justice comes calling, we had better answer "here I am!" For it is God calling, and we must be responsive, responsible. By the same token, conservative, orthodox, and right-wing religious types have to watch out that their willingness to specify and determine in well-formed formulae *what* they love when they love their God does not turn into an easy irresponsibility and complacency, which allows them to think that since they have signed on to some creedal formula or the other, or done what they were told to do by the creedal handbooks or leaders, they have done their duty and carried out the depths of their *responsibility*. Then the relatively determinate character of their confession of faith becomes a convenient answer, which substitutes for responding "in spirit and in truth" (John 4:24).

I am groping for a genuinely *religious* idea of "truth" and a true idea of "religion," one that turns on troubling about oneself and about what one loves, on allowing oneself to be unhinged and troubled by the impossible. *Inquietum est cor nostrum*: Our hearts are restless and they will not rest until they rest in you, O Lord, my God. But who are you, Lord? And where are you? And who am I? I am saying that the structure of the religious breaks into our lives just at that point where we experience the limits of our powers, potencies, and possibilities and find ourselves up against the impossible, which is beyond our powers. Those who refuse the religious want to retain their own self-possession, their own power, their own will. The ancient Stoics said that if we seek what is possible, accept what is necessary, and stay within our limits, we shall have autonomy and autarchy; then we shall be happy because we shall not lack anything that we let ourselves desire. Augustine mocked that idea by saying that the happiness of such men is to have made peace with their misery! The Stoics were advising us to refuse religion, to refuse to make ourselves vulnerable, to have calm and *apatheia* (no passion), whereas in the religious sense of life all that calm is disturbed by a divine passion, a divine *perturbatio*, a divine unhinging, a restless stirring with a passion for the impossible. Remember that St. Augustine's famous "conversion" did not exactly lie in giving up sex and romance, which was only its most sensational side, but in giving up his disposition over himself, his attachment to his own career and ambitions as a rising rhetorician who stood to get a comfortable and important post in the Roman government. His conversion occurred at the precise point when his self-possession was displaced by a possession by

God, when his love of self gave way to a love of God. It is only when he had broken the spell of self-love – you know that I love you, Lord – that he was visited by the question, but *what* do I love when I love my God? So long as he was pursuing his own desire for the flesh and his own ambition, there was absolutely no question at all about what he was after. Augustine's conversion lay in a transformation of what he loved, which involved a self-transformation of Augustine himself into a question unto himself, and a transformation of his love into a question about what he loved.

This deep and resonating question of what he loved when he loved God was not a question he was asking in the abstract or prior to the love. It was not as if he had been invited to speak on this topic at a conference and the sponsors had offered to pay him a handsome honorarium and to pick up his expenses, so he felt that he had better come up with something. "God" was not some sort of grand theoretical or explanatory hypothesis for Augustine, like the much-sought-after "unified theory" for scientists today, but something that had transformed his life. The question he asked about love was a question he raised *within* love, within the passion of his love, in which he tried to understand what he *already loved*. It was when the love of God began to overtake him and unhinge him and shake his life to the roots that the question, what do I love when I love you, O Lord, began to have some teeth in it. We usually think that we first have to get to know something or someone in order subsequently to get to love them. But one of the great lessons of St. Augustine's writings is that it is love that drives our search to know. Caught up in the grips of what is loved, love is driven to understand what it loves, which is something that we shall see borne out below when we turn to St. Anselm, whose thought is very close to Augustine's. Love both drives the question and makes it possible to understand what we love, as far, at least, as it can be understood.

In the religious sense of life we passionately love something that resists any Final Explanation, that refuses to be boiled down to some determinate form. Contrary to the way his orthodox readers like to read the *Confessions*, I think that Augustine's story shows us that religion kicks in, not necessarily when we sign on the dotted line of some *confessional* faith or other, but when we confess our love for something besides ourselves, when (on one etymology) we "bind ourselves over" (*re-ligare*) to something *other*, which means something other than ourselves, or (on another etymology) when we gather ourselves together (*re-legere*) and center ourselves on a transforming focus of our love. Something grander and larger than us comes along and bowls us over and dispossesses us. Something overpowers our powers, potencies, and possibilities, and exposes us to something impossible. Something makes a demand upon us and shakes us loose from the circle of self-love, drawing us out of ourselves and into the service of others and of something to come. The religious sense of life kicks in when I am rigorously loyal, "religiously" faithful (*religio* on still another etymology, meaning "scrupulous" or "in a disciplined way") to the service of something other than myself, more important than myself, to which I swear an oath, which has me more than I have it.

Even if we do not have a lot of clarity about exactly what this is. *Especially* if we do not. Only then am I driven to question and to ask what I love. I am driven by love to understand what I love when I love my God. I am at the very least in love with love, not in the sense that I love being in love, love flirtation without commitment, courtship without marriage, sex without children, but in the sense that I am beset by love, overtaken by love, drawn out of myself by love. I understand that the whole idea of a self rests in this dedication, this gift of myself, to something beyond my own self-love – to the children, all the children, not just my own, to the future, to the least among us. In the name of God, or justice, or the Force, or something, I know not what. Even if, if to all the world, I look like a garden-variety atheist (if you still move around within the increasingly questionable distinction between theism and atheism). Perhaps especially then.

I am not making a brief against the confessional faiths. The religion of the churches and the organized faiths remains, for better or for worse, the dominant form that religion takes today and the permanent depository of the most ancient religious narratives. They provide religion with a critical mass, with a structure and social constancy without which it would likely disappear or dissipate. They provide permanent structures – buildings and institutions and communities – within which the great narratives are preserved, interpreted, and passed on to the next generation. They perform innumerable acts of service and generosity and they preserve the name of God by proclaiming it and praising it systematically and consistently. They also devote an ungodly amount of time to bringing order to their ranks, silencing the voice of dissenters and excluding – "excommunicating" – those who beg to differ from their communities and institutions, doing battle with those of different confessions and in general trying to make people who do not agree with them look bad. So the people of the impossible are also impossible people, a point that I will take up in the fourth chapter. It was always thus (small comfort, that).

Institutionalized communities are defined by their identity

and by the power to maintain their identity, which includes the power to excommunicate the different. If the community is hospitable to too many "others," it will cease to be a community. Hospitality, welcoming the other, is something that religious institutions passionately preach but practice with a carefully calibrated caution. Any wider sense of religion, of a religiousness without the confessional religions, including our religion without religion, will always be parasitic upon the confessional forms, will always feed off them, repeat them with a difference, all the while depending upon the worldly body and the spiritual voice that these institutions give to religion.

I am not arguing against the confessional faiths but only insisting that they ought to be disturbed from within by a radical non-knowing, by a faith without faith, by a sense of the secret, and that they ought to confess like the rest of us that they do not know who they are. *Quaestio mihi factus sum* is a good institutional model, not just something for the privacy of the heart. It would always be a matter of inhabiting the distance between the concrete and determinate religious faiths, Islam or Catholicism, say, with their vast creedal and institutional armatures, their bishops, their mullahs, and their occasional armies, and this more radical and open-ended religion that does not know what it believes, that does not have the wherewithal to lay down its head, that is made a question unto itself, that does not know what we love when we love our God. Faith is not safe. Faith is not faith all the way down, so that all the gaps and crevices of faith are filled with more faith and it all makes for a perfect, continuous and well-rounded whole. Faith is always – and this is its condition – faith without faith, faith that needs to be sustained from moment to moment, from decision to decision, by the renewal, reinvention, and repetition of faith which is – if I may say so –

continually exposed to discontinuity. Faith is always inhabited by unfaith, which is why the prayer in the New Testament makes such perfect sense, "Lord, I do believe, help my unbelief" (Mark 9:24). For my faith cannot be insulated from unbelief; it is co-constituted by unbelief, which is why faith is faith and not knowledge. For I do not know what I love when I love my God. Not that I do not love God, for that is not a matter of knowing, but that I am always asking who or what the God that I love is.

We are social and historical beings, concretely situated in one historical, cultural, and linguistic tradition or another, formed and forged by one religious tradition or another. Our religious aspirations have been given one determinate form or another by the traditions to which we belong and by which we have been nourished, by the way the name of God has been given flesh and substance for us. I do not deny that; I affirm that. I have no desire to twist free from such historical situatedness in the name of some purely private religion or of some overarching ahistorical universal religious truth, which would be the religion of an *Aufklärer*, of an intellectual with a feeling of superiority over garden-variety believers. A God without historical flesh and blood, a religion without the body of a community and its traditions, is a bloodless abstraction. But I want these determinate forms of religious life to be inwardly disturbed by the secret that springs from their historical contingency, put into question by the question of what they love, and forced always to negotiate the distance between the determinate historical form in which their religious desire has taken shape in them and the open-endedness of the secret, of the equally religious confession that we do not know who we are or what we love when we love our God.

The Christian, to take the example I can work with the best, is someone who confesses that the power of God is with Jesus, that Jesus is Emmanuel, which means "God with us," and at the same time, in the same breath, is continually disturbed by the question that Jesus asks, "who do men say that I am?" (Matt. 16:15). Contrary to the condensed wisdom of the bumper stickers, Jesus is not The Answer but the place of the question, of an abyss that is opened up by the life and death of a man who, by putting forgiveness before retribution, threw all human accounting into confusion, utterly confounding the stockbrokers of the finite, who always seek a balance of payments, which means who always want to settle the score. Who is this man who counsels us to forgive, to give up what is our due, who asks, who did, the impossible? What does his life and death tell us about ourselves, including those among us who, because of an accident of birth, have never heard his name? What is happening in and what is opened up by our memory of Jesus, by the mystery of his unaccountable teachings of forgiveness and who told us to be of a new heart (*metanoia*)? What is contained in our memory of Jesus that cannot be contained by all the accumulated prestige and power of the institutions and structures, the creedal formulae and the theologies, that dare speak in his name? What mystery unfolds there? The mystery of the love of God, to be sure. But what do I love when I love my God?

Where would I be without my tradition, without my worn-out copy of the *Confessions*? I do not know what questions I would ask, or what texts I would read, in what language I would think, or in what community I would move about. But I make a brief against the "closure" of the confessional faiths, against allowing them to close the circle of faith, to slam shut the doors of faith from the intrusions of other faiths or of un-faith, to keep faith behind closed doors, safe and secure, and thus to suffer the illusion that there is some way to settle the question whose very meaning is to be unsettling and that arises from our unsettled, unhinged, and "unquiet" (*inquietum*) hearts. It would never be for me a question of choosing between a determinate religious faith and this faith without faith that does not know what it believes or who we are, but rather of inhabiting the distance between them and of learning how to let each unhinge and disturb – and by disturbing, deepen – the other. For just as faith needs always to be exposed to the faithlessness of confessing that we do not know what we believe, or what we love when we love our God, so this more open-ended and indeterminate love of God cannot subsist in a vacuum, cannot occupy some timeless, ahistorical, and supra-linguistic spot above the fray of time and chance, some pure desert of indeterminacy. On my accounting we ought to pass our days slipping back and forth between the two, giving the desert of the secret its due while all along seeking out the hospitality of our historical traditions and the shelter of our culture, without which we would simply perish. We might think of ourselves as desert wanderers, *homines viatores*, on the way we know not where, but continually finding respite and hospitality in the determinate faiths, even as the safety of these shelters is haunted by the unsettling thought of the searing desert sun and numbing desert nights that lie outside their sheltering circles.

All this talk about the impossible has only recently become possible again. It has for too long been declared off limits – by "modernity," by the "Enlightenment," by the great "masters of suspicion," Marx, Freud, and Nietzsche, who proposed to unmask it as so much displaced "libidinal desire" or "alienated consciousness." But contemporary philosophers have grown increasingly weary with the "old" Enlightenment. Their tendency has been more and more to unmask the modernist unmaskers, to criticize the modernist critiques, to grow disenchanted with the disenchanters, to question modernity's prejudice against prejudice, and to look around for a *new* Enlightenment, one that is enlightened about the (old) Enlightenment. That has inevitably led to a break within their own ranks on the hot topic of religion, where even otherwise "secular" intellectuals have become suspicious of the Enlightenment suspicion of religion.

That explains my use of St. Augustine in these pages, and my invocation of the story of the Annunciation to the Blessed Virgin. I am taking advantage of this moment that is sometimes called "post-modern." One of the most important things this word would have meant had it not been ground senseless by overuse is "post-secular." (One other very important thing that it means, or would have meant, is post-industrial, high-tech "virtual culture," which I shall discuss in the next chapter.) In this so-called post-modern moment we can listen to great and weepy saints like Augustine without dismissing them as twisted souls casting furtive glances at their mommy. But I hasten to add that this "post-secular" frame of mind is not uncritical or naive. It has arisen as the result of an "iteration" process that by criticizing the critique ends up in a *post-critical* position, one that is interestingly like but importantly unlike the *pre-critical* position. The result is the unearthing of a certain analogy between the pre-critical and the post-critical and newly opened lines of communication between them. But this is only an analogy, because the post-critical will have also passed through the critique and taken it to heart, even if it has moved on.

Thus it is important for me to tell my story about how the secular world became post-secular, albeit in a highly condensed thumbnail sketch that is unashamedly intent on driving home a point. For this is the story of how the impossible has recently become possible, and it goes to the heart of my argument. A good history is never just a story but is always an argument, for every history worth its salt is telling us who we are (we who do not know who we are). In what follows I will speak of modernity and of its "before" and "after," which for simplicity's sake I entitle the "sacral" age, the age of "secularization," and the "post-secular." But I solemnly warn the reader to be extremely uneasy about any such easy periodization for, hero that I am, I accept no responsibility for it.

THE SACRAL AGE

In the eleventh century, at the onset of a rebirth of learning in the Middle Ages, St. Anselm of Canterbury, a great admirer of St. Augustine, wrote a book entitled *Proslogion* ("allocution"), which he described as an exercise in "faith seeking understanding" (*fides quaerens intellectum*). He begins this treatise with a prayer that asks God to help him find God, to teach him where and how to look for God. *Where* are you, Lord? If I have wandered far away from home and have gotten lost, I ask *where* my home is. I have no doubt that it is there, but the question is where and how shall I find it? Like Augustine's *Confessions*, Anselm's inquiry clearly moves in a circle, from God to God, asking God to help him find God, like a blind man asking someone to keep talking so that he can follow the sound, on the good Augustinian principle that love seeks to understand what it already loves. The God whom Anselm seeks is a party to the search, implicated in the very undertaking to find Him, expected to help, indeed to lead the search and to give the seeker signs, for the seeker's attention is distracted by worldly cares and his mind is darkened by sin. The *Proslogion* thus does not describe a movement from a cognitive degree zero to infinity, but from a groping and confused sense of something or someone, somewhere, to a clarified sense of who and where. It describes a movement from God to God and in God, who lights the way. Had someone suggested to Anselm that he break out of this circle and start from scratch, from some neutral point outside the circle, Anselm would have thought him mad (or a fool). For Anselm, outside the circle there is no light and nothing happens.

It is teasingly difficult to choreograph this scene and to lay out the space of Anselm's little book. We have to get comfortable not only with the fact that he is turned toward us, face forward, giving us a frontal allocution, *pros-logion*, confronting us with a proof, but also with the fact that we have come upon him at his prie-Dieu, his back to us, his face aglow with prayer and turned to "You," O Lord. He shifts easily between "God," a massive theological object, a big metaphysical word with a thunderous semantic punch, and "You," a word whispered to a lover, ever so softly, tenderly, lovingly, the most loving word in our language. "You" is not a spoken "meaning" at all but an address to another person, to an interlocutor rather than about something allocuted. We must imagine a yearning and tormented lover sighing, "where are You, my Beloved?" "How long will You turn Your face from me?" That adds still another twist to the scene. For if Anselm's face is turned toward God in prayer, God's face is turned away from Anselm, and Anselm seeks, if not to see the countenance of God, at least to be seen by God, to have God turn His face to him and look down upon him and hear his prayers.

It is in this context that Anselm propounds one of the most tantalizing and frequently discussed "arguments for the existence of God" in the history of philosophical theology, one that makes it into all the anthologies. After having propounded a number of lesser arguments for God's existence in a previous book, Anselm seeks here one single, overarching, irresistible argument that God really exists that would just sweep us away and bring us to our knees in prayer and praise and admiration for God's mighty ways. The famous argument is that if we look within ourselves and determine what we mean by the God in whom we believe, we shall find that what we mean is "that than which no greater can be conceived," as any fool (insipiens) would agree. By a fool he means, not someone with a low IQ, but someone who mixes up the finite and the infinite, who mistakes the uncreated for the created, and who says that there is no God. But even this fool knows what he means by the God who he says does not exist and would agree that this is the idea that he has in his mind. But that than which no greater can be conceived cannot exist merely in the mind, for then anything that really exists outside the mind would be greater than it. From this it follows that God, that than which no greater can be conceived, must needs exist not only in the mind but also in reality, lest something greater than God be conceivable.

Many commentators who have been drawn down the labyrinthine corridors of this argument have never been heard from again. I am not about to add myself to their number, although, were I to do so, the last word you would have heard from me before I disappeared into the abyss would have been an objection that the argument was not formally valid; I would thereby have added my voice to that of Thomas Aquinas, who did not like the formal argument any more than I do, and he was a saint. I am not a saint and I am more interested in the choreography of the scene than the logic of the argument, in the context of a believer seeking understanding, who asks God to give understanding to his faith so that he may better understand what he already believes and so better love what he has come to understand. I am interested in Anselm's idea of God as one who must exist just because God is so perfect, so plentiful, so really real, and so excessive, an idea Anselm has drawn from a religious experience that is bathed in God's bountifulness and that respects the incomprehensibility of God. Anselm has a self-delimiting concept of God, a concept that points to the inconceivability of what it conceives, to the excess of God beyond the concept.

The point that interests me – the choreography – is that Anselm is conducting this argument on his knees, in a loving reverence and a faithful love of the God beyond God, of the God of his experience beyond the God conceived in any concept. He finds God within himself and he finds himself within

God, and then seeks to clarify what he believes and finally concludes by giving thanks to God – to "You" – for helping him to understand what he believes.

SECULARIZATION

Things could not have changed more dramatically when this argument was rehearsed in the seventeenth and eighteenth centuries. Whether Anselm's argument is defended or rebutted in modernity, the choreography is ignored, all the candles are blown out, and the animating religious spirit has been drained out of it. The prayers and tears of St. Anselm are replaced by dry-eyed, bare bones logic. The monastery chapel, the spare but gorgeous Gregorian chant, and monk's prie-Dieu have all disappeared. The argument is labeled by Kant the "ontological" argument, by which Kant means an argument that proceeds not from empirical or experimental data but from pure a priori ideas. But that is the *last* thing it is for Anselm, for whom it was washed ashore from an ocean of religious experience, from his inner Augustinian experience of God's bountiful goodness and excess which he seeks to clarify and glorify. What has happened in the intervening six or seven centuries is that philosophers from Descartes to Kant have constructed the idea of "consciousness" and the conscious "subject." The old Augustinian idea of the "self," this sinful, self-questioning, passionate, prayerful, weepy being, of restless heart and divided will, has been displaced, although you can still find it on the margins of modernity, e.g., in Pascal and later on in Kierkegaard, as we shall see. In its place we find a sovereign, self-possessed, dispassionate "thinking thing," fully in charge of its potencies and possibilities, surveying the contents of its mind to sort out which among them represents something objective out there in the external world and which should be written off as merely internal and subjective.

Another way you could describe what had happened is to say that in the meantime somebody has invented "religion" and declared it off limits from "reason." In the Middle Ages the word *religio* was a word for a virtue, the habit of being religious, of tending to one's duty to God "religiously," that is, with a sense of rigor and scrupulous loyalty to God, with a love of God. That is the sense of religion that I am defending. *Vera religio* meant being genuinely religious, like being truly just, not "the true religion" versus "the false religion." But there was no separate sphere or delimited region called "religion," which was to be differentiated from reason, politics, art, science, or commerce. All the masters and practitioners in these several fields of endeavor were in varying degrees religious or irreligious, loyal to or cynical about their religious obligations. The church was, to be sure, a massive institutional presence, and popes certainly waged sometimes epic battles with kings. This sense of living in a Christian world – or a Muslim one – pervaded everything. Christianity, Islam, and Judaism were all over the place, covering everything, seeping into every crevice, constituting the very air everyone breathed. But it is for just that reason that "religion" in the modern sense, as some *separate* sphere, apart from the "secular" order, did not exist. The word "secular" did not describe a sphere separated from "religion" but referred to someone who was not a member of a monastic order. The "secular masters" in thirteenth-century Paris would have been greatly disconcerted had this term been taken to imply that they were not religious. Nor would anyone have thought to describe the anonymous architects who dedicated their genius to the design and construction of towering cathedrals, or the anonymous artists who painted murals based on the life of Christ or the stories in the Jewish Scriptures, as "religious" artists, since that would not have differentiated them from anybody else. They were just architects and artists, and their work was to make biblical life visible and palpable to the faithful, just as the work of the clergy was to dispense the sacraments. It was not until the Renaissance that "secular" subjects began to appear, one of the earliest of which is the fourteenth-century fresco in Sienna entitled *Allegory of Good Government*, depicting scenes of civic order and a peaceful countryside without any overt "religious" subject matter.

So by the time it gets to Kant, Anselm's argument for the being whose bountiful excess Anselm experiences daily, in prayer and liturgy, in community and everyday life, has been transplanted to a different world where it is transformed into an argument about whether existence is a predicate. We cannot conclude to the existence of something S simply from the definition of S, Kant argues, because a definition is a set of predicates and existence is not a predicate. That can be seen by considering that there is not a dime's worth of difference between the idea of a *possible* hundred dollars and the idea of a hundred dollars that *actually exists*; there is not a penny more or a penny less in the mere thought or definition of a hundred dollars than in the thought of a hundred dollars actually posited in the pockets of our trousers or deposited in our account. The only difference is that in the latter situation the conscious subject has grounds to "posit" the actual existence of a hundred dollars, but not in the former. Existence has to do with "positing" some S that is a complex of predicates, but it is not itself a predicate.

Next case.

We have entered a world composed of thinking, rational

"subjects" charged with sorting through their sensations and ideas to separate out those among them that "represent" genuine "external objects" from those that are merely internal subjective mental events. Before modernity, it was the opposite. The medievals regarded "inanimate" things (without a soul or *anima*) as "contracted" to themselves, while beings possessed of a soul overflow their bodily limits and reach out into ("intend" or "tend into") the world. The philosophers of medieval and ancient times did not think of knowing as the "internal event" of representing external things; instead, they thought of knowledge as an act by which the soul embraced the whole world – the soul is in a way all things, Aristotle had said – and formed a unity or sameness with it (*idem fieri*). The soul is always and all along opened out upon the world even as the world has always and all along taken possession of the soul. The task was not to break out of an internal prison into the external world but to clarify the vague and unclarified contact with the world in which we are all along immersed.

But the moderns took their lead from the "new science" and the way that Galileo set measurable mass, velocity, and spatio-temporal position on the "object" side, while setting sensations like "red" or "warm" on the subject side. When, following Copernicus, he also put the measurable movement of the earth around the sun on the object side and the perceptual experience of the sun's "rising" on the subjective side, he set the agenda for the philosophers of the Enlightenment to see just how far that sort of subject–object sorting could go. The Church then decided that it had inside information that God preferred Ptolemy to Copernicus. Galileo was a devout man and a serious Catholic, but the Church started a war with him, and thus with modern science – it had found no cause to wage war on St. Albertus Magnus, one of the greatest scientists of the Middle Ages – that it would lose and lose badly, because it could not tell the difference between a contingent historical construction and the mind of God.

So, in modernity, the question of God is profoundly recast. Instead of beginning on our knees, we are all seated solemnly and with stern faces on the hard benches of the court of Reason as it is called into session. God is brought before the court, like a defendant with his hat in his hand, and required to give an account of himself, to show His ontological papers, if He expects to win the court's approval. In such a world, from Anselm's point of view, God is already dead, even if you conclude that the proof is valid, because whatever you think you have proven or disproven is not the God he experiences in prayer and liturgy but a philosophical idol. Is there or is there not a sufficient reason for this being to be?, the court wants to know. If there are reasons, are they empirical or a priori? Are they good or bad? That is what the court has assembled to decide. What does the defendant have to say for himself? What's that you say? Nothing but a few hymns, some pious prayers, and a bit of incense? Whom can he call in his defense? Shakers and Quakers and Spirit-seers all in heat? Next case!

The metaphor of the "court" of reason is one of the pervasive features of Kant's quintessential formulation of modernity and Enlightenment. Modernity has a powerful sense of jurisdiction, of the need to settle questions of law, *quid juris*: with what right may we say that *S is P*, and whose domain or jurisdiction is it to do so? As well as questions of fact, *quid facti*: what are the objective data? Do we have empirical studies? The moderns have a rigorous sense of boundaries, limits, and proper domains, and they make everything turn on drawing these boundaries neatly and cleanly. They insist on drawing sharp lines between subject and object, consciousness and the external world, science and religion, faith and reason, public and private, rational and irrational, empirical and a priori, cognitive and non-cognitive, fact and value, is and ought, descriptive and normative, sacred and profane, religious and secular. In making these discriminations, they made or invented the very categories they were discriminating, none of which had existed, and certainly not in these precise terms, before modernity. While the communication of the soul with God, with "You," could not have been more "intimate" to Augustine and Anselm, they would have been astonished to hear that it was therefore subjective, private, and non-cognitive. Augustine said if you want to find God, the most real and transcendent being of all, do not go outside, but remain at home, within the soul. If you go in (intra me) you will go up (supra me). While Augustine and his successors certainly distinguished faith and reason, they treated this distinction like markers or milestones along a continuous path of upward ascent, marking off stages in a continuous movement of the entire community. They did not think of them as two separate and discrete spheres or domains, disjoined from each other as the internal from the external and the private from the public.

This all comes to a head in Kant's "three Critiques," his critical discrimination of the lines to be drawn among knowledge (the true), ethics (the good), and "aesthetics" (the beautiful), which constituted a critical delineation of the domain of "Reason." To these three he adds, in a later book, the space that can be carved out for "religion within the limits of reason alone." For Kant, to take one example, the "work of art" is the occasion of a subjective feeling of beauty, but it is deprived of any "truth" content. That would lay the foundations for a later aestheticism, art for art's sake, and the image of the Bohemian artist, an image that the great commissioned artists of the Renaissance would have found baffling. The modern art gallery is a testimony to the power of the discriminations Kant made and reinforced. Here numerous works of art, from many different times and places, hang on the wall to be passed in review before an aesthetic subject who looks them over on weekends (if they have a timed ticket). The art gallery is a characteristically modern institution, where art is detached from the rest of public life and made into a picture for the pleasure of a subject-viewer, while the art of the ancient and medieval world melted into their life of politics and prayer. Kant's "three Critiques" produced the effect of an archipelago that left us all island hopping from science to ethics to art. In religion, Kant said, we take the moral law, which is the voice of Reason, also to be the voice of God. So God does not get his own island but must build his temple on the island of ethics. That means that we should distinguish the rational element in religion, which is its universal ethical content, from the superstitions, supernatural dogmas, and cultic practices which vary from one religion to another.

When Lessing wrote Nathan the Wise, he dramatized a good Enlightenment point. In response to a trap question put to him by Saladin, the Muslim Sultan of Jerusalem, about which faith is the one true religion, Christianity, Judaism, or Islam, Nathan, a wise Jewish merchant and diplomat (Lessing's stand-in for Moses Mendelsohn), tells the Sultan a parable about three rings (Act III, sc. 7). Three sons are given identical rings, one of which has the power to make its owner beloved of God, but since none of the three is sure which ring has this special power, the only way each son can prove his claim to have the authentic ring is to lead an exemplary ethical life that makes him truly worthy of God's love. The three rings represent the three great religions of the Book, all of which are equally true in the eyes of God.

If we go back to our characterization of a religious person as someone who has made a pact with the impossible, then we can say that Kant is a policeman who patrols the borders of the *possible*. Indeed, Kant is the Chief of Police. Kant is always telling us what is possible and what is not, always laying down the conditions of the possibility of this or that, of science or art, of ethics or religion, and all along trying to contain them rigorously within their borders. That is why he is so deterministic about science, moralistic about ethics, and aestheticizing about art, and why he shrinks religion down to ethics. There are no fuzzy edges or blended shades in Kant's world. He does not allow these spheres to interpenetrate each other and he has no interest in opening them up to what lies beyond their horizon of possibility, to the impossible. Eventually, when this all got a little boring and you told him about the impossible, he would accuse you of what he called *Schwärmerei*, a kind of irrational exuberance which proves that you are a little mad. (Which of course we are, but with a divine madness, which is vastly to be preferred to the sanity of German philosophers. But that is to get ahead of my story.)

OUR PROPHETS: KIERKEGAARD AND NIETZSCHE

Hegel rightly thought that the oppositional, dichotomizing way of thinking of modernity that had come to a head in Kant was a mistake, and he put it to the torch. He thought that Kant was trading in "abstract" concepts of the "understanding," thin, one-sided, formal schemata that dissolve into the richer unity of concrete life. He thought that Kant's "moral law" was a formal and empty morality for morality's sake that acquired content and teeth only in the concrete ethical and social life of an historical community. He criticized Kant's predilection for timeless a prioris for failing to see that reason's necessities unfold in time, that universals require the body of particularity to develop, that eternity needs time in order to spread its wings. By insisting on the historically situated character of reason, and by criticizing the abstract and ahistorical thinking of Enlightenment rationality, Hegel was clearly on to something. But Hegel never questioned Kant's Enlightenment idea that reason is a "system," which led Hegel to argue that the historical process was governed from within by a law of Divine Reason. Hegel trumped Kant's abstract "understanding" with historical "Reason," which is the power to apprehend the convergence of opposites in the concrete historical world, and to see that history is the autobiography of God in time.

But every time that Hegel said that Christianity painted a beautiful religious "picture" of which he was delivering the hard-core "conceptual truth," that his philosophy was "Christianity" raised up to the level of Reason, Kierkegaard howled in pain. In a series of passionate, brilliant, and witty pseudonymous works, Kierkegaard complained that the God of Abraham and Isaac had not come into the world in order to get an account of himself from German metaphysicians. In contrast to the apostolic age of Christianity, the pseudonyms complained, when it took the courage to face the lions to call oneself a Christian, today the whole world (they meant Western Europe) calls itself Christian. In "Christendom," a term of abuse Kierkegaard used to describe a world with too many philosophers and too few lions, where everyone thinks they are Christian, the essential task is to get beyond Christian faith to Reason, the System, philosophical Truth. But, as "Johannes de Silentio" objected, far from surpassing father Abraham, he has spent a whole life trying without success to get as far as the fearsome and awesome faith, the fear and trembling, that accompanied the patriarch up to Mount Moriah.

It is with Kierkegaard, I would say, that the "post-" in what we call post-modern or post-secular or post-metaphysical first surfaced. Against the "System," Kierkegaard took his stand with the "singular individual" – for the God of the Scriptures has numbered every hair on our head and counted every tear, and God prefers the single lost sheep to the ninety-nine safely in the fold (the "millions"). By refocusing us on our own religious purity of heart, Kierkegaard brings us back to Augustine, back on our knees before God, *coram deo*. The external worldly "results" of our actions are in God's hands. History is not the story of the Eternal unfolding rationally in time, but the mind-numbing event of the altogether astonishing intervention of the Eternal into time in the Moment of the God-become-man, a crashing of the party of reason and history by the God who assumes the form of a servant, which scandalizes the Jews and confounds the philosophers.

Back in the middle of the twentieth century, we honored Kierkegaard as the "father of Existentialism," whereas today a good many "post-modernists" number him among their prime progenitors. Kierkegaard is the whistle-blower, the bleeding individual being chewed up by the Philosophical System who first shouts "Enough! Somebody get me out of here!" Out of the nineteenth century, out of World History, out of Absolute Philosophy! Kierkegaard was being driven mad by all this Reason, suffocating from all this Absolute Knowledge. Like the author of the Letter to the Romans, his brilliant and caustic pseudonymous authors do not think that the world makes sense, or that human beings could lift themselves up by the bootstraps of their own Philosophical Reason, or that the soundness of the Moral Law would make us whole. He thought that the opening monologue in the first scene of Shakespeare's *Richard III* – "I that am rudely stamped, and want love's majesty . . ." (Act I, sc. i) – was worth more than all the moral theories of the philosophers, which have not the slightest idea of the terrors of existence. We have all been wounded by existence like children by a cruel step-mother, and ethics makes sport of us. He took existence to be a gaping wound whose bleeding can be stanched only by a transforming leap of faith, which is why, in my opinion, one of the predecessor figures of one version of "post-modernism" is St. Paul.

For Nietzsche, on the other hand, the apostle Paul headed up the list of people who never would be missed. It never fails to amaze careful and sympathetic readers of both Nietzsche and Kierkegaard – it takes a certain type to pull that off – how deeply convergent and yet how wildly divergent their views are. Nietzsche is the other nineteenth-century predecessor figure of the post-modern situation, the other voice desperately crying help, the other academic outsider and renegade philosopher who took the world to be a wild and untamable vortex. Like Kierkegaard, Nietzsche was a brilliant stylist who broke the mold of philosophical propriety by writing in a madly beautiful, bitingly witty, and unnervingly aphoristic style that could not live within the academy, who added another famous pseudonym, "Zarathustra," to the likes of "Johannes Climacus" and "Johannes de Silentio." Both were miserably unhappy and tormented geniuses who wrote with their blood; had they ended up happily married, with three children, and tending their lawns on weekends, we would likely never have heard a word from them. They had made pretty much the same diagnosis of the nineteenth century as the advent of "mass man," as the triumph of the bourgeois middle class, with its accompanying mediocrities – mass values, mass reading habits, mass thinking (or thoughtlessness), and the disappearance of singularity and passion. They were both made green around the gills by the mediocrity of "Christendom," by the leveling effects of mass media, and they practically predicted the emergence of the mediatized culture of the American suburbs today.

But they prescribed radically different remedies for recharging the intensity of passion and the courage for singularity in the increasingly moribund culture of nineteenth-century Europe. For Nietzsche turned to Dionysus, not Christ, to the ecstasy of aesthetic pleasure, not the passion of religious faith. Kierkegaard would have agreed with Nietzsche that "God is dead," that the life has gone out of European faith – that is pretty much what defined "Christendom" for Kierkegaard – but he sought to restore this life by wandering the ancient streets of old Europe holding the New Testament over his head and shouting Augustine's *tolle, lege.* Just take this Book and read it, anywhere you choose to begin, and you will see that the comforts of bourgeois Christendom are everywhere contradicted by the true demands of evangelical life, for Christian life is the way of the Cross, the immense difficulty of the passion of faith that needs to be reaffirmed from moment to moment. Do not be comforted by the thought that you have been baptized or have signed your name to the Nicene Creed. That is no different than the pagans who thought that they could be saved by Philosophy, or the Jews who thought that they were saved by the Law, or anybody else who has been duped into thinking that the world makes Sense. We are not supposed to earn a comfortable living off the Crucifixion; we are supposed to be crucified to the world.

Nietzsche, on the other hand, thought that if you took the New Testament in hand, you should wear gloves so as not to be contaminated by it. Nietzsche had a terrifying vision of the world as so many forces swirling and sweeping their way across infinite cosmic space, building up and discharging their energies, forming unstable constellations that soon enough come undone. We ourselves are proud little animals, stationed on a distant outpost in some remote corner of the cosmos, who have no stomach for the cruelty of the cosmic play. We require a tidier view of the world than is suggested by all that tumult if we are to get ourselves through the day. So we invent the categories that we need, words to simplify the forces and a grammar to organize them for us, like the "ego" or "self," "cause" and "law," along with distinctions that inspire us and give us guidance, like "truth and falsity," "being and appearance," or "good and evil." These are all signs we have made up and sunk into the surface of the forces, so many fictions of grammar we have devised, like a veil we weave and then lay over a visage too hideous to behold. But these words have no purchase on the forces, and underneath this veil of grammar the forces continue to play themselves out. Soon enough the distant planet spins itself out and falls back into its sun and the little animals have to die, disappearing without a trace. Then the forces draw another breath and continue their dance across an endless cosmic sky.

In both Kierkegaard and Nietzsche, the world is a chaotic tumult, a senseless game into which we did not ask to be entered. Why was I not consulted about being born?, one of the Kierkegaardian pseudonyms asks. Where is the manager to whom I can make my complaint? In both Kierkegaard and

Nietzsche, the figure of the God torn to pieces holds center stage. For Nietzsche, "Dionysus" is not a god governing the world but a god of the world and its life-cycles, the god of the vine cut back to the stem every fall only to be reborn in the spring, the god of the festival, of cyclical rebirth, of the endless circle of life and death. He who truly says yes to life does not do so half-heartedly, with his fingers crossed, trying to take the good without the bad, life without death, joy without suffering. Rather, he says yes to the whole of life, without subtraction, attenuation, or substitution, the whole wheel of becoming, life and death together, for each is linked to the other in a golden chain. For Kierkegaard, the god torn to pieces is Christ, and Him crucified, whose sacrifice of blood washes over us and redeems us from this body of death and sin, a transcendent God who has come down into the world and assumed our flesh, which He has allowed to be pierced and torn, in order to lift us up with Him when He comes again at the end of time.

In Kierkegaard and Nietzsche, the world of Enlightenment Reason and of Hegelian Absolute Knowledge is left far behind. They each foresee in his own way the madness of the twentieth century, a century whose genocidal violence made a mockery of Hegel's sanguine view of history as the autobiography of the Spirit in time. That is why the twentieth century took them as its prophets. Kierkegaard and Nietzsche sketch the lines of a world after the Enlightenment, after Hegel, after Philosophy, writ large. For after the fury with which Kierkegaard bit into the hide of German metaphysics, and after the way that Nietzsche told the tale of how the "Real World" that the philosophers conjured up had become a "fable," no one would dare write Philosophy large again.

By the end of the nineteenth century God was indeed all

but dead among the intellectuals. Religious faith had become scientifically dubious (Darwin), psychoanalytically twisted (Freud), and economically and politically reactionary (Marx), while Kierkegaard was saying that Christian faith represented a leap into the Absurd. The view from the pews was largely unshaken by all this. Modernity had no spiritual vision to offer in the place of the one it had torn down, which is perhaps why religion still prospered among the poor and uneducated rank and file in the churches. But religion was dead or dying fast among its learned despisers who confidently predicted that it was destined to disappear as science progressed and the general level of learning rose.

But it just did not work out that way.

DESECULARIZATION: THE DEATH OF THE DEATH OF GOD

The status of God and religion had undergone a deep transformation in modernity. Failing to meet the muster of "objective" proof and demonstration, religion was lodged deep in the domain of subjectivity. There it was either considered safe and sheltered from the harsh lights of its critics and cherished by those who nourished religious faith as something that belongs to the realm of the "heart," or it was written off by the heartless, hard-nosed scientifically minded as some kind of purely private buzz. "Faith" now stood in much sharper contrast with "reason" than could ever have been imagined by the authors of the Confessions or Proslogion, who viewed their books as an exercise in fides quaerens intellectum. Reduced to a thinner, more emotive phenomenon, more a matter of an interior commitment or existential passion, faith had little or no purchase on the nature of things. What had disappeared under the guns of modernity was the robust faith of the medievals where fides and intellectus, the love of learning and the love of God, went hand in hand. The middle term, an inner lining of metaphysical or speculative theological reason – and our own St. Augustine was the crucial player in the formation of this lining – that moved confidently between metaphysics and prayer, had melted away under the heat of modernist criticism. Uniting the spirit of Greek metaphysics with their biblical faith, the medievals – Christian, Jewish, and Islamic – were just as at home with thinking philosophically about God and God's relationship with the world (including even detailed accounts of the "spiritual substances," angels) as they were at prayer.

Now in my efforts to reinstate a dialogue with pre-modern thinkers, I do not think that we can get the old metaphysical style of arguing that the medievals cherished back on its feet. I have not given up on philosophy, but I take philosophy to be a phenomenological, not a metaphysical or speculative enterprise, that is, I steer its nose close to the earth of concrete description. Besides, if we go back still further, *before* the medieval age of faith seeking understanding, back to the world of the Scriptures, we find a situation in which faith flourished but *without* the metaphysical back-up, without the thick carpet of metaphysical rationality upon which faith and reason could curl up with each other in medieval times. Indeed, St. Paul took great delight in berating Greek philosophers about the futility of their speculations and urging upon them the need for what Kierkegaard, who was going back to Paul, called the leap of faith. So clearly this lack of a robust metaphysical theology was no impediment to faith and religion; it was a characteristic of biblical faith, both Hebrew and Christian. The metaphysical theology had come later, when Christianity, having become the established religion of the Roman Empire, had come to terms with Hellenistic learning, a program that had first gotten off the ground with Philo Judaeus back in first-century CE Alexandria. That made possible a phenomenon like "Christian Neoplatonism," which is the world to which Augustine belonged. But neither Jesus nor Paul, neither the early apostolic communities nor the rabbinic tradition before them, had a head for "metaphysics," which was a Greek idea – whence Tertullian's famous question, "what does Athens have to do with Jerusalem?".

That produces an interesting effect, a fascinating mirror play between the earliest biblical and apostolic age and what fairly secular continental philosophers have recently been calling "the deconstruction of metaphysics" or "overcoming metaphysics," in which we see a certain recuperation or repetition of the pre-metaphysical situation of faith. That puts Nietzsche and St. Paul on the same page, at least on this point (which would certainly have given Nietzsche one more of his famous migraines). Nietzsche had argued for the historical contingency of our constructions, the revisability and reformability of our beliefs and practices, all of which, as he said, are "perspectives" that we take on the world and that have emerged in order to meet the needs of life. Of course, he used that argument to torpedo what he called the "Christian Platonic" tradition, the unholy wedding of two great despisers of the body (some wedding night!), under whose cruel rule, he complained, the West has suffered too long. In that respect, Nietzsche's thought can be joined up with that of Marx and Freud as part of the continuing Enlightenment critique of religion, a further extension of the argument for secularism. But any such supposed alignment of Nietzsche with the Enlightenment – a ruse that Walter Kaufmann employed for years to make Nietzsche look good to the Anglo-American philosophical establishment at Princeton – is inherently unstable and bound to come unstuck. Marx and Freud always insisted (to the point of protesting too much) that they were "scientific" thinkers. But Nietzsche thought that science was just one more version of Christian Platonism, that the death of "God" implies the death of "absolute truth," including the absolutism of scientific truth; physics too is a perspective. Nietzsche was trying to argue that Christianity was crucified on its own Cross: by insisting that God is truth and hence on the need for the faithful to be truthful, Christians ought finally to be brought to the point of honestly and truthfully confessing that Christianity too is another fabrication. But a surprising thing happened on the way to the death of God: Enlightenment secularism *also* got crucified on the same Cross, and that spelled the death of the death of God.

Nietzsche's argument boomeranged in a way that nobody saw coming. What the contemporary post-Nietzschean lovers of God, religion, and religious faith took away from Nietzsche was that psychoanalysis (Freud), the unyielding laws of dialectical materialism (Marx), and the will to power itself (Nietzsche) are *also* perspectives, *also* constructions, or fictions of grammar. They are *also* just so many contingent ways of construing the world under contingent circumstances that eventually outlive their usefulness when circumstances change. That is, Marx and Freud, along with Nietzsche himself, find themselves hoisted with Nietzsche's petard, their critiques of religion having come undone under the gun of Nietzsche's critique of the possibility of making a critique that would cut to the quick – of God, nature, or history. Enlightenment secularism, the objectivist reduction of religion to something other than itself – say, to a distorted desire for one's mommy, or to a way to keep the ruling authorities in power – is one more story told by people with historically limited imaginations, with contingent conceptions of reason and history, of economics and labor, of nature and human nature, of desire, sexuality, and women, and of God, religion, and faith. All these reductionistic critiques of religion turn out to be, on Nietzsche's own account, more varieties of what Nietzsche called the "ascetic ideal," a belief in a rigorous and unbending order of "Objective Truth." For Nietzsche's assertion that "God is dead" had a wide sweep that included Absolute Truth, Physics, and the Laws of Grammar, anything that tries to hold the center firm. The declaration of the "death of God" is aimed at decapitating anything that dares Capitalize itself, which included not just the smoke and incense of the Christian mysteries, but anything that claims to be the Final Word. That had the amazing and unforeseen effect of catching up hard-ball reductionistic and atheistic critiques of religion in its sweep.

The danger here is that what would emerge from this Nietzscheanized historical critique is an "anything goes" relativism – nothing is true, everything is possible, one belief or perspective is as good as another. That danger was not always resisted by the "academic left," which Allan Bloom grumpily but accurately called the "Nietzscheanized left," those lovers of Nietzsche who headed in the direction of an aestheticized view, not only of art, but of science and ethics, which made them vulnerable to the objection of relativism. That is why I insist that the "post-secular" style should arise by way of a certain *iteration* of the Enlightenment, a continuation of the Enlightenment by another means, the production of a New Enlightenment, one that is enlightened about the limits of the old one. The "post-" in "post-secular" should not be understood to mean "over and done with" but rather *after having passed through* modernity, so that there is no danger of the emergence of an irrational relativistic left, on the one hand, or of a lapsing back into a conservative pre-modernism masquerading under the guise of post-modern, on the other, which is the sort of thing that is going on right now in a "post-secular" movement that describes itself with the unnerving, angry, and resentful title "Radical Orthodoxy." Radical Orthodoxy is a good deal more orthodox than radical, has managed to convince itself that God came into the world in order to side with Christian Neoplatonism against post-structuralism, and appears utterly dumbfounded by the fact that medieval metaphysics has lost its grip on contemporary thinkers. A more enlightened Enlightenment is no longer taken in by the dream of Pure Objectivity, even as it deploys a new idea of reason that is no longer taken in by the illusion of Pure Reason. It has a post-critical sense of critique that is critical of the idea that we can establish air-tight borders around neatly discriminated spheres or regions like knowledge, ethics, art, and religion. By carefully tweaking modernity, we can give it a post-modern twist.

So far be it from me to say that modernity and secularization were a bad idea. As beautiful as the *Proslogion* is, the philosophical texts of those days are devoid of the voice of women and they are silent about the world of serfs that supported them from below. Augustine spent a lot more time fretting over stolen pears than about the fate of his unnamed common-law wife, from whom he severed himself at the time of his conversion. Heaven protect me from lamenting the break-up of a top-down trickle-down hierarchical conception of power or the break-up of deep metaphysical systems that tried to lend the weight of Being or of God to purely contingent political orders and historically contingent philosophical and theological formulations of the traditional faith.

That is why it is always the Augustine of the *Confessions* that I invoke, the intensely personal story of the conversion of a man of prayers and tears, not his more metaphysical ruminations and not the *City of God*, where the bishop in Augustine comes out swinging.

I am not prepared to dismiss Descartes, who started something that led to the most modern idea of all, the idea that in a way defines modernity: that we have the right to say what we think, to think what we want, to publish what we think, to think or publish or doubt or believe *anything*, without fear of censorship, excommunication, exile, or execution. The only limits on such rights are the rights of others to do the same and to enjoy the same freedoms. The only criteria for evaluating such beliefs are their plausibility and capability of surviving in a public debate. That's the defining idea of modernity, the light of the Enlightenment, and I love that idea very much. The post-modern idea, if that is a word we can still employ, which casts a shadow on all that light, is to insist that we all understand that a free and public debate and the unforced force of pure reason are also fictions and hence that they do not guarantee fairness or a good outcome, not by a long shot. That idea I *also* love (a good mind, it has been said, is one that can cling tenaciously to two contradictory ideas). That is because wealth, educational advantages, linguistic, historical, cultural, and nationalist prejudices, racism, sexism, and the influence of special interests inevitably distort public debates, public elections, and public space generally, which is always curved in somebody's favor. The post-modernists do not have a better alternative except to suggest that we try to conduct public debates, in politics and academies, in the full realization that there is no such thing as an undistorted perspective and try to correct for that. There is no unforced force of pure reason or ideal speech situation, no view from nowhere or timeless ahistorical answer; there is no one right answer to most questions. There are many different and competing beliefs and practices and we should make every reasonable effort to accommodate them, to let many flowers bloom.

Including the flowers of religion. For what no one saw coming was the way the Nietzschean critique undoes the modernist critique of religion and opens the doors to another way of thinking about faith and reason. The result of a more sober reading of Nietzsche is not relativism and irrationalism but a heightened sense of the contingency and revisability of our constructions, not the jettisoning of reason but a redescription of reason, one that is a lot more reasonable than the bill of goods about an overarching, transhistorical Rationality that the Enlightenment tried to sell us. For that is a highly unreasonable Reason, a hyper-enlightened illusion that no one can live up to. No one foresaw that Nietzsche's theory of fictions would converge with the biblical critique of idols, of mistaking our own graven images for the divinity. In this way of looking at things, the Enlightenment and its idea of Pure Reason are on the side of Aaron and the golden calf, while Nietzsche, God forbid, he who philosophizes with a hammer, stands on the side of Moses as a smasher of idols, and stands right beside Paul giving the Corinthians holy hell about the idols of the philosophers. That opens the door for a notion like the love of God, the idea I love most of all, to get another hearing among the intellectuals. For it is a bald Enlightenment prejudice, unvarnished reductionism, to try to run that idea out of town and to denounce it as sucking on your thumb and longing for your mommy. The name of God is the name of the impossible, and the love of God transports us beyond ourselves and the constraints imposed upon the world by what the *Aufklärer* called "reason" and Kant called the conditions of possibility, transporting us toward the impossible. Today, Marx, Nietzsche, and Freud are all dead but God is doing just fine, thank you very much.

In the wake of Nietzsche and many others – Wittgenstein and Heidegger foremost among them – philosophers today have largely rejected the idea that there is some proud over-arching thing called "Reason" and they have settled instead for the humbler idea of "good reasons," in the plural and in lower case. Their idea is not to reject reason but to redefine and historicize it as a historically contingent "take" we have on things – which makes it look a lot more like "faith" – the best one available at the time and the one we go along with until we are forced to revise it by some unexpected turn of events. These philosophers have a more modest sense of how far our concepts cut, a heightened sense of the difficulty of things, and a sharper sense of knowledge as a more open-ended, fluid, mobile, less logo-centric undertaking. Knowledge for them does not require freedom from presuppositions, but it is seen as uniquely structured by presuppositions that should be as supple and fertile as possible. They think that disciplined learning in the sciences and the humanities has a lot more to do with the insights and instincts of the well trained, the suggestions and questions of the initiates, imagination, a measure of good luck, and an ability to cope with an utterly unexpected turn of events than with the much-vaunted "method" of modernity. Their idea of "reason" looks a lot more like what Aristotle called *phronesis*, which means the practical good sense to know how to apply relatively general and empty schemata in very concrete circumstances, allowing for the differences. They have a sharper ear for the "other" and the anomaly and a sharper sense of the prison house of the "same," that is, of the way "I," "we," and "our" tend to be traps set for us by an inherited way of thinking and doing things. They have not jettisoned philosophy but have taken up philosophy in a humbler, uncapitalized condition, pursuing more modest philosophical projects. They do not think that there are rigorous borders between faith and reason, public and private, subject and object, politics and science or religion, but that these things have a disconcerting way of running together and that it is an artifice to try to separate them too stringently.

Philosophers have largely rejected the idea that there is some overarching meta-language (say, the language of atomic sub-particles) into which the various particular languages can be translated and adjudicated and they have taken up the idea of what Wittgenstein dubbed "language games." There are multiple games, each with its own internal rules of consistency and meaning, each of which serves a different end. On that telling it would be a mistake to try to translate or to reduce one game to the other, to reduce what is going on in a prayer, for example (which clearly belongs to an especially religious language game), to the terms of economics or psychoanalysis. Something would surely get lost in the translation (namely, the prayer).

Philosophers have largely rejected the idea that there is some overarching meta-narrative, some vast "story" of what is going on in "Western" history, like the old story of the emancipation of the masses (Marx), which is the left-wing version of Hegel's "History of the Spirit," or the latest version, the end of history as the triumph of the free-market economy (Francis Fukuyama), which represents the right-wing version of Hegel. They denounce such stories as "totalizing" and they are more inclined to see history in terms of innumerable little narratives, competing stories that throw the big picture into question (which is why I distrust my own story about pre-modern, modern, and post-modern as too clear, too neat, too "totalizing"). They keep an eye out for the little ones, the voices and languages and peoples of the past that were ground up in the Big Story that history tells, which tends to be the story told by the winners.

What interests me is how, after the big guns of these great philosophical warships from Plato to Hegel grew silent, the still small voice of religion could once again be heard. Nowadays we even find important "secular" philosophers like Jacques Derrida and the late Jean-François Lyotard attending once more to the prayers and tears of St. Augustine, not to mention Heidegger, whose *Being and Time* was in no small part inspired by the Tenth Book of the *Confessions*, or French feminist philosopher Luce Irigaray meditating on the "divine" – all in search of the God who comes "after metaphysics." To the great astonishment of learned despisers of religion everywhere, who have been predicting the death of God from the middle of the nineteenth century right up to Y2K, religion in all of its manifold varieties has returned. Even to say that is misleading, since religion was reported missing mostly by the intellectuals; no one outside the academy thought that it had gone anywhere at all. Religion has returned even among avant-garde intellectuals who have given it a new legitimacy by discrediting its discreditors, suspecting its suspectors, doubting its doubters, unmasking its unmaskers.

The flower of religion is one of the blossoms in our post-modern anthology.

In this little treatise *On Religion*, which is turning out to be a treatise *On the Impossible*, I have been arguing that the impossible has recently become possible again, that the very force of modernist criticism when turned on itself opens the way for a post-critical and post-secular posture that accommodates the passion for the impossible. That movement of living on the limit of the possible, in hope for and expectation of the impossible, a reality beyond the real, which I take to be the mark of a religious sensibility, has survived the secularizing and reductionistic critiques that have been directed against religion for the better part of the last two centuries.

But the world described by this much-abused word "post-modern" is also "post-industrial." The setting in which the contemporary religious sensibility finds itself has been dramatically altered, not only from the pre-Copernican world of the Scriptures, but even from the Newtonian world of chunks of matter in motion. We live and hope and pray and weep in a world of high-tech advanced telecommunication systems, a dizzying, digitalized world that is changing everything. Yet far from falling prey to the prophets of the death of God, far from dying a digitalized death, the divinity simply takes on new digitalized high-tech life. Religion shows every sign of adapting with Darwinian dexterity (to use an analogy that would give the fundamentalists no comfort), of flourishing in a new high-tech form, and of entering into an amazing symbiosis with the "virtual culture."

The reason for this, in my view, is that, far from undermining religious sensibilities, the advanced communication technologies are actually trading in religious goods and thus provide a new space, a cyberspace, for religious imagination. For if, as I have been arguing, religion disturbs our sense of reality and leaves us a little unhinged, if it causes our pre-set sense of the real and the possible to tremble by exposing us to something *hyper-real*, then the communications revolution going on in our midst, with its accompanying sense of "*virtual reality*," which gives us the power to "visit" distant "sites" in cyberspace with the click of a mouse, is laced with *religious* implications. We have begun, God help us, to tamper with our sense of what is real. But is that not what every religious figure from the Jewish prophet to the televangelist has dreamed of doing? To break the grip of material actuality and open our eyes to being otherwise, to a dimension beyond reality that lifts the limits imposed upon us by presence and actuality – is that not something that classical religion has been trying to do ever since Moses took a hammer to Aaron's golden calf, which tried to contract the transcendence of God to a physical object?

But how is it possible to love the Most High while also loving high-tech and relishing technology's spectral, virtual, surreal effects? What inner communication transpires between theophilia and technophilia, angels and computer technologies, religion and the internet companies whose daily feats are recorded in the volatile Nasdaq composite index? No one saw this coming. This is not the way the death of God squad thought things would turn out! What is going on? In heaven's name!

If the philosophers were investment counselors, we would all be broke. As we saw in the previous chapter, they have been confidently assuring us ever since the nineteenth century that God is dead, or will be quite soon. At the very least, they say, the divinity is not feeling very well and can hardly be expected to last out the week. But here we are at the dawn of the twenty-first century and religion is alive and well. The old bumper sticker has come true. "God is dead – Nietzsche. Nietzsche is dead – God." The various confessional faiths continue to flourish, not only in third-world and underdeveloped countries, where there are days when the only thing you think you can do to improve your lot is to sink to your knees and pray for divine intervention, but also in the United States, where, according to the polls, the vast majority (some 95 percent according to some studies) of the most prosperous people the world has ever known profess belief in God.

Religious faith is flourishing in all its varieties, from the elbow-patched tweedy membership of the American Academy of Religion to everyday life in the pews and parishes to the spine-tingling religious experiences reported by the guests on *Oprah*. An astonishing number of people profess to believe in angels, in addition to which not a few mention believing in UFOs, alien abductions, and "channeling." Indeed, even the entertainment industry has had its hopes raised by numerous sightings of Elvis (none confirmed as yet). The TV show *Touched by an Angel* is a success in the ratings, and *The Celestine Prophecy*, a book that tells us that we should treat coincidences as marks of divine intervention, was a national bestseller. Most people believe in heaven (and, predictably, most people also believe that they are going to heaven!). Authorial envy prevents me from observing that

Stephen King's tales of preternatural events have made him a millionaire many times over. Anyone with a taste for such things can regularly hear remarkable stories about all sorts of paranormal events and interventions in the lives of the people who are guests on the daytime TV talk shows. Visit any of the large-chain bookstores, like Borders or Barnes and Noble, and you will find almost as many books on angels (check the "New Age" section) as you will find on how to run the latest version of Microsoft Windows. For the people buying these books, the angel in Luke's nativity story is not a standard literary vehicle in a religious narrative (the word just means "messenger"), which is what scriptural scholars will tell you, but the proper name of a spiritual entity who will answer to the proper name "Gabriel," if he has ears (and if he is a "he," which would require having something else). A recent search I conducted of Amazon.com under the subject "angels" yielded 2,416 titles, all of which could easily be fitted on the head of an electronic pin (microchip). Furthermore, you can instantly purchase any one of these books with a click of a mouse that sends a signal across cyberspace with the speed of light or of – well – a disembodied spirit to a virtual bookstore which "contains" millions of books!

So we are faced with an amazing – shall we say an impossible? – situation: the simultaneous flourishing of science and religion, and indeed, at its extremes, of advanced hardball science along with some far-out screwball superstition. We live in a world where the most sophisticated scientific and high-tech achievements cohabit not only with traditional religion but also with the most literal-minded fundamentalisms, New-Age spiritualities, and belief in all sorts of bizarre, hocus-pocus phenomena. One has to wonder, of course, how deeply, if at all, some of this cuts into the lives of these people, whether any of it stays hatred, anger, and dishonesty or elicits generosity and love in daily life. But the wave of religiosity is not confined to the fringes. Most people believe in God and a good many of them associate themselves with the traditional confessions, although the proliferation of so much other strange and untraditional stuff going on makes one wonder if the traditional structures are going to hold up. To be sure, to a certain extent this wild proliferation of the strangest beliefs does not refute but confirms the death of God. For the name of God as the name of the transforming future, as the name of justice for the least of God's children, is indeed dead as a doornail in books like Deepak Chopra's *The Seven Spiritual Laws of Success*, which instructs us about the pursuit of wealth based on the venerable spiritual principle that greed is good. I shall come back to the vacuity of this wave of superstition below, but I am at present more interested in pursuing the amazing symbiosis of religion and techno-science in the post-secular world.

According to the nineteenth-century positivist philo-sophers, none of this, traditional or fringe, mainstream or off the map, should be going on by now. The rapid growth of science and technology was supposed to spell the end of the old God. So why has not the swift progress of scientific research induced a pronounced scepticism about spiritual entities instead of co-existing with a prosperous spirituality industry? (And a prosperous industry it is; capitalism, bless its heart, if it has one, knows very well that there is a market there!) Why is it that both the various traditional faiths and various far-out practices are flourishing (while nobody reads the philosophers)?

I see all this as a continuation of the case against modernity, of the delimitation of modernity that I sketched in the preceding chapter. When it comes to religion, the two opposing camps of modernity – the Enlightenment and Romanticism – have both been proven wrong. As we have just seen, recent philosophy has become disenchanted with the disenchanters of the forest, distrustful of those hard-nosed men of the Enlightenment who were sure that religious fantasies were like mushrooms that would perish in the light of scientific rationality. But the Romantics, who represent the flip side of the Enlightenment, who warned us about the destructive hybris of the march of science and technology – Mary Shelley's *Frankenstein: Or, the Modern Prometheus* (1818) was one of its most popular moments – were no less mistaken. The Romantics feared and lamented the "flight of the gods" under the onslaught of modern technology, a point that was pressed in the twentieth century by the German philosopher Martin Heidegger. But Heidegger and the Romantics were both thinking of the filthy "smokestack technologies," not the "clean," spirit-like post-industrial high-tech world that is as light as an electron and requires no more effort than a click of the mouse. The old-fashioned opposition of technology and religion was forged in the dusty mines and grimy factories of the industrial revolution, not the virtual world of post-industrial cyberspace, where the main menace to our health is not black lung disease but carpal tunnel syndrome, caused by sitting in front of a computer all day.

Today, when we hitch a ride on the electronic circuits that form the invisible ribs of a vast virtual world we soar like pure spirits, sailing effortlessly and with breathtaking speed across staggering distances. We make a mockery of the "old" idea of "matter," a clunky, hard, dumb, dense stuff that takes up space and sits around waiting to be moved by a mover (Aristotle) or that just keeps on moving mindlessly until something stops it (Newton), but in either case lacks the wits to act on its own. Today we are learning how to get rid of matter, which is fast going out of style, and replacing it with a more subtle idea, with the idea of a more subtle stuff, rather the way "the Force" in *Star Wars* – I shall return to this point shortly – simply eludes the spirit/matter disjunction. The resolution of the mind/body debate that has kept philosophers employed for two and a half millennia will turn on seeing that both conscious life and material bodies are a function of a more subtle third thing that is not quite matter or spirit.

We no longer need real physical retail stores in order to shop for merchandise, or need to haul our bodies laboriously around from place to place in search of the best price on a new car, or to trot off to the library, trekking up and down staircases and rooting among voluminous and dusty shelves to find a book. Not when we can surf the web in seconds and order a book with a click, or even just download text from an electronic data-base. The storied *Oxford English Dictionary* is now "on line," while anything needed by patristics scholars, a hoary lot, if ever there was one, is a click away on their computers in the vast resources of the *Patrologia Latina* and the *Patrologia Graeca* on line. Even the old *Encyclopaedia Britannica* has been compressed to a flow of electrons in cyberspace, replacing the imposing physical presence of dark oak bookcases filled with all ninety volumes that testified so conspicuously to the dedication of affluent suburban parents to their children's educational well being (which also solves the problem of how to divide the volumes after the divorce). Today, when you hit a bit of hypertext in a text, you are invited to spread your cybernetic wings, to leave the page you are reading, to lift yourself beyond the limits of the room in which you are seated, to sail across the seas, to enter an old library or to explore some distant "site" which is but a point and click away. We can, without moving our gross and heavy bodies an inch, sail swiftly across space and enter the Louvre, summon up old Latin manuscripts in distant libraries, or hear the voices and see the faces of the people we are writing about on our word-processing systems.

We carry cell phones around whose signals easily penetrate thick walls and link us instantly across continents and wide oceans while we stroll through shopping centers or try to steer our cars with one hand (the accident rate, not surprisingly, is rising). These satellite technologies have bled into our sense of space: they awaken a living and working sense of a revolving planet rotating around the sun and they disturb our innate pre-Copernican sense of a flat immobile earth. We email people all over the world in different time zones without so much as licking a stamp. We are gradually being relieved of the grossness of material reality by waves of electrons racing hither and yon, sweeping us off to distant places on the other side of the round earth, up and down unimaginably small silicon and neurological circuits that support our computers and our conscious life and that extend our dense and heavy bodies into infinity, or so it seems. We have broken the contraction of our bodies to the ground beneath us and to the containing space that surrounds us and we have allowed them to fly through space at electronic speed. If Heidegger liked to quote the line from the German Romantic poet Friedrich Hölderlin, "poetically does man dwell upon the earth," we today get a bigger surge out of sailing cybernetically around the earth.

We have divined a way to mime the angels who intervened to spring the apostles Peter and Paul from jail (Acts 5:19; 12:7) and to render our bodies into ethereal wisps that pass through the solid substance of walls like the risen Jesus visiting the frightened disciples. The old debate between mind and matter is fast becoming as antiquated as a debate about the relative merits of various sorts of fountain pens. "Matter" is going out of style. The electron is turning out to be the Cartesian "pineal gland" which mediates in the obsolete opposition of mind and matter as the lines between these two antagonists in the ancient dualism are blurred by the electronic revolution. More and more we live our lives in a kind of virtual, spectral spirit world – if we are prosperous enough to own a computer, which is a point I shall revisit below. (Nobody sleeping under a bridge has brought along a laptop to check the latest Dow-Jones average.) Matter is on the way out and materialism is for technophobes who are afraid to buy a computer. We jog and exercise not only for our health but in order to reestablish contact with our embodiment, to reassure ourselves that we still have a body. We still get sick and die, which is a big reminder of embodiment, as big as it gets, but we are working on that. By the end of the twenty-first century the killer diseases of today will have gone the way of diphtheria; vital organs will be routinely harvested and replaced, and average life spans will stretch out to a century and beyond. Then we shall get to work on reversing the internal time clock in cellular life so that our bodies will not age. (After that, professorial tenure will become a really serious problem.) So, far from turning us all into materialists, the revolution in electronic communication systems has begun to weaken the distinction between the "virtual" world and the "real" or "material" one.

The death of God squad did not see this coming. How, secularist intellectuals ask themselves, can people who use cell phones and email, who enjoy the benefits of advanced computer technologies and who fly from continent to continent on powerful jets, swallow biblical ideas like the Virgin Birth or the Resurrection, believe in spiritual entities like angels and the devil, or lose sleep over the threat of everlasting punishment for their sins in a lake of unquenchable fire and sulphur? And that is the *traditional* stuff. What about all the non-biblical things, like sightings of Elvis and channeling? How can televangelists make use of advanced communications satellites orbiting around the earth to preach a fundamentalist gospel that commits them to believing that the world is squatted firmly on its haunches in the middle of the universe – "You set the earth on its foundations, so that it shall never be shaken" (Ps. 104:5)? Do these people not see that if the bodies of Jesus or the Virgin Mary really had physically "ascended" into "heaven," as the evangelists put it with their pre-Copernican imaginations, then they would still be up there in orbit alongside our communication satellites and might very well have been spotted by now? Had those bodily ascents happened two millennia later, would they not have required an air traffic controller to clear their take off? How can an age that is about to complete the human genome project also witness the removal of evolution as a mandated subject in the high-school biology programs in Kansas, all in order to make room for teaching creationism and a story about how we all descended from two people who were talked into eating forbidden fruit by a conniving serpent? How, the intellectuals wonder, do people today let such ideas get inside their heads? Why is God not dead, which is what was *supposed* to happen? Why has God not gone the way of Ptolemaic astronomy?

Part of the answer, I am arguing, is that the advanced communication technologies actually undermine old-fashioned materialism and deprive the material world of its rigid fixity and dense and heavy substantiality. The impossible has its techno-scientific analog in the utter transformability and permeability of physical things in a world that is mastering the genetic map and is digitalizing everything. In the film The Matrix, the premise is that the human population at large was living in a virtual world of computer-induced images and controlled by an alien species that was harvesting human beings for its own life purposes. The philosophical premise is actually quite similar to George Berkeley's famous argument in the eighteenth century that esse est percipi, that the being of the world is its being perceived, or, to give his Latin a contemporary rendering: the being of the world is a function of the software that is running, of the sort of information-processing system in place. Berkeley argued that the world is nothing but a flow of images unfolded before our minds, not by a great and powerful computer run by a devious alien species, but by a great and powerful and good God. (It was from wrestling with Berkeley's argument that we derived the "tree falling in the forest" conundrum.) Berkeley was an Irish Protestant bishop and he offered this argument as a critique of the growing threat of materialism posed by the "new science." But the new new science (and the new Enlightenment and the new Nasdaq-centered economy) is on the side of the bishop, not of the materialists (who belong to the old Enlightenment). For in the advanced communication technologies the world we perceive is very much as his Eminence argued, namely, the effect of the information-processing system we use, which renders the matter versus spirit distinction unstable and even slightly obsolete.

That, I contend, is one part of the answer. The other part has to do with the "de-secularization" process I described in the preceding chapter, the suspicion we have acquired of Enlightenment suspicion. Secular intellectuals, poor things, cannot win for losing. Even as contemporary philosophers move more and more beyond the modernist, critical, and reductionist habits of thought that grew up in the old Enlightenment, which was keyed to the old new science, the new technologies have simply created the opportunity for a new religious imagination. But before assessing where all this leaves us, before drawing the moral of the story of how the secular world became post-secular, which I shall undertake in the next chapter, I suggest that we take a break and take in a film – one that illustrates for us what religion might look like in "another galaxy, another time," which tells us more than a little about this one, here and now.

THE RELIGION OF *STAR WARS*

Our point of departure in this essay on the impossible is Gabriel's startling "Annunciation" of the Incarnation to the Virgin Mary, and Mary's famous "fiat," which forms a centerpiece of Christian faith and the subject matter of the exquisite murals of Fra Angelico and countless other works of art over the centuries that have worked this scene deeply into the imagination of Christians of all times. Now far from trying to make this or similar stories look bad, the latest installment of *Star Wars – Episode I: The Phantom Menace* – reproduces a high-tech version of this ancient Christian narrative in which the impossible happens, again. In George Lucas's intergalactic version of Luke's nativity story, there is a high-tech holy family, a "virgin birth" and blessed mother, a child with a human mother and fathered by a heavenly power, all of which is part of a piece of a popular science fiction that is laced with religious import and trades on religious structures.

Far from serving as a vehicle for debunking religion or exposing it as pre-scientific superstition, the enormous popularity of Star Wars over the years derives in no small part from its reproduction of elemental mythic structures and its transcription of classical religious figures into a high-tech world. Whether the traditional churches like it or not, films like Stars Wars are the way a good many young people (who teach their parents about how to run the family computers and program their VCRs, but are frequently ignorant about the basics of traditional religion) get their "religion" today (even as sport is the way they and a lot of other people get their "art"). In my daughter's college dorm, one of her roommates had hung a poster that read – very tellingly from my point of view – "All I need to know about life, I learned from Star Wars." Then it proceeded to itemize what Immanuel Kant would have called "maxims of prudence" like "Anger, fear and aggression lead to the dark side," "In seeking you destroy, patience is your ally," "In your pursuit of peace and justice, the Force will be with you always." The advice is ancient but the packaging is new. While no one would argue that Star Wars represents a new religious classic, and no one is likely to mistake Luke Skywalker for the Messiah, the truth is that Star Wars reproduces classic mythic, ethical, and religious figures, both Western and non-Western, in a compellingly contemporary form that has the effect of a vast high-tech Odyssey, one that will, when completed, include three trilogies ("omne trinum perfectum est," Augustine said).

The old pre-Copernican cosmology in which the traditional religious stories were cast has utterly lost its grip on our imaginations, and that has inevitably altered how we think about "religious transcendence." As we have seen, it is starting to make very little sense to look "up" to "heaven above," or to think of Jesus "ascending into heaven," when what the heavens harbor for us is a system of communication satellites and hordes of jet airplanes (most of them over-crowded and late). Although we still experience the sun "rising," we are pretty fully settled into the Copernican turn and we do not use pre-Copernican and agrarian images to make a religious point. That is what New Testament scholar Rudolph Bultmann saw very clearly when he said that we have to "de-mythologize" the New Testament – that is, get past the old cosmology – if we want it to make religious sense. But Bult-mann did not see *Star Wars* coming. For one of the points that is nicely illustrated by the example – and there are many examples to choose from – of *Star Wars* is that religious tran-scendence is not debunked or de-mythologized in *Star Wars*: it is redescribed and re-mythologized. The structure of religious transcendence is clearly to be found there, but without the dualities of classical theism – between matter and spirit, body and soul, natural and supernatural, science and faith, earth and heaven, time and eternity.

The Phantom Menace tells the story of the origin of the epic battle between the Republic and the forces of darkness, which looks a little bit like a sci-fi version of the battle between the Kingdom of God and the Prince of Darkness. Here the virgin birth, taking a dark twist, issues in "Darth Vader." Of course, genes (or midi-chlorians) will tell, so the virgin mother is also the virgin grandmother of Luke Skywalker (a rather heav-enly family name and a given name that recalls both George and the third gospel) who takes on father Darth and the death star. "Darth Vader" (dark + death + star + invader) is a diabol-ical figure, a bad angel, a menacing "messenger" (*angelos*) and bearer of evil, an elemental figure of evil, who has gone over (*vadere*) to the "dark side," which he visits upon the Republic, that is, upon us. The image is imported directly from Joseph

Campbell's *Hero with a Thousand Faces*, which describes a classic mythic scenario in which the hero does battle with a mysterious figure of an Evil One who, unbeknown to the hero, turns out to be his own brother – or here his father. In medieval tales, Campbell says, this figure comes clad in black armor with a black helmet shielding his face from view. Like every Evil One worthy of the name, he is the figure of good gone bad. Anakin Skywalker, a youngster (an only child) with an actual mother but whose father is the Force (a classic mythic figure: earthly mother, heavenly father, except this is not earth and the Force is not in "heaven"), is a wonderfully likeable lad, a remarkably precocious, brave, and gifted youngster, and neither we nor the virgin mother can be expected to foresee what lies in store for him. Qui-Gon Jinn and, after Qui-Gon's death, the young Obi-Wan Kenobe, can be forgiven for trusting their Jedi instincts and mistaking him for the "chosen one" (the Anointed One, the Messiah), prophesied in Jedi Scriptures long ago to bring balance to the Force. The Jedi Council – fatefully right on this point – contends that Qui-Gon found the young man too late to tame the passions that already stirred within him. "There is already too much anger in him," Mace Windu objects. "Clouded this boy's future remains, Obi-Wan. A mistake it is to train him," says Yoda in an extraordinary expression of disagreement with a decision of the Jedi Council (not to mention his extraordinary word order). This anger and aggression would eventually overtake Anakin and lead him over to the "dark side," a phrase that sends a shudder through the youngsters who repeat it with gravity and a perfectly straight face. Like Lucifer and the other bad angels, the "Powers and Principalities" who prowl the earth seeking to make trouble, whom Christ will conquer (Rom. 8:38; I Cor. 15:24), Darth Vader and the other "Sith" lords (Sith: sin + sinister + sick) – Darth Maul (that does not sound good) has horns and a red face – are beings of preternatural gifts gone awry. They have allowed the flow of "the Force" to be diverted from good to evil. They remind us (well, at least some of us) of Aristotle's description of the *deinos*, the terrible, strange, and uncanny one who uses brilliant talents for evil ends.

The war in *Star Wars* does not transpire between two equal but opposed Forces but turns on a disturbance or lack of balance within the one and only Force. *Star Wars* is distinctly anti-Manichean. The Kingdom of God, or the messianic age, or the rule of peace and justice, depends upon the smooth and harmonious flow of the Force, while war rages when the Force is disturbed or distorted. Thus the war between good and evil is waged between the Sith lords who make the Force an instrument of their own evil intentions and the Jedi knights who make themselves an instrument of the Force, allowing the Force to flow freely and harmoniously, to follow its natural rhythms, undistorted by anger, fear, and aggression. But if the Force is with us – this draws on classical religious and mystical formulae like St. Paul's "I live, now not I, but Christ lives in me" (Gal. 2:20) – that means that I allow the Force to flow freely through me without distorting it by my own ego. The greeting "The Force be with you" is a transparent transcription of ancient religious hymns and liturgical formulae like *dominus vobiscum*, "The Lord be with you," reproducing one of the most sacred greetings we can give one another, "God be with you," "may God protect and watch over you," "may God hold you in the palm of His hands." Had St. Paul been a character in *Star Wars* he would have expressed his love and admiration for Jesus not by calling him the coming Son of Man but by spreading the word around the galaxies that "the Force is with him" (Emmanuel, God with us). But the Force is not God, not a transcendent creator of the visible heavens and earth, which is a pre-Copernican figure, but a pervasive mystico-scientific power that runs through all things. The basic religious schema of *Star Wars* is rather more Eastern than Judeo-Christian.

The "Jedi" knights, who serve the Force, are the protectors of the Republic, guardians of the Kingdom of God, God's knights, like crusaders or members of a religious order ("Jedi" sounds a little like "Jesuit"), dedicated to the service not of the pope, to be sure, but of the Force. They wear dark brown robes reminiscent of habits worn by members of a religious order, but they are again, like a lot of things in *Star Wars*, rather more Buddhist than Christian votaries. Initiates are trained by masters, "mind to mind," as they say in the Buddhist tradition. They trek across the galaxies with an inner calm, peace, and recollection that reminds one of a Buddhist monk and they can spring into action with the deadly Force of a Buddhist archer or jujitsu fighter. They spread out their hands over their enemies like a biblical exorcist or healer in an attempt at mind control. Does this man heal by the power of God or of Beelzebub (Matt. 12:24)? Their link with the Force gives them preemptive instincts that warn them of what their opponent is going to do before he does it, which is very handy indeed! For someone who knows a little something about the history of religion, the art of Jedi fighting is very reminiscent of Eugen Herrigel's classic account in *Zen and the Art of Archery*. The Zen master must learn to proceed by instincts deeply buried beneath the level of the conscious ego; the skill of the master archer is not a matter of having a great eye, or great hand–eye coordination. Rather "it shoots" within him. This eradication of the eye of the ego, of the ego's conscious intentional life, is so radical that when "it shoots," the Zen archer's arrow will hit its target even if the archer is blindfolded. The Jedi mission is to bring peace not just "on earth," which is a pre-Copernican formula for our religious aspirations and still stuck in an outdated cosmology, but throughout the universe, by letting the Force flow, letting the Force be with us all across endless galaxies, establishing an inter-galactic peace throughout the Republic, in a stunning expansion and realization of the "Kingdom of God."

We notice that in *Star Wars* there are no churches, synagogues, temples, or mosques as such, that nothing like the traditional religions is to be found, and that there is evidently no traditional priest class. When Qui-Gon Jinn is killed by Darth Maul, his body is cremated after being held in state in the Jedi Temple, which is not a church but something like a rotunda in which the bodies of heroes are honored. The cremation rites are attended by Anakin, Obi-Wan, Queen Amidala, Supreme Chancellor Palpatine, the Jedi Council, and others, but there is no mention of a priest, a religious liturgy, or a properly religious ceremony. The body is turned to ash and instead of personal immortality or an afterlife Obi-wan softly consoles the sobbing Anakin with the thought "He is one with the Force, Anakin. You must let him go . . . he is gone." From the Force, with the Force, back to the Force. The Force gives and the Force takes back. The Force is first, last and constant, alpha and omega, like a great seamless matrix, undivided by the opposition of body and soul, matter and spirit, this life and the next.

But that does not mean that there is no religion in *Star Wars* or that the whole universe has succumbed to an inter-galactic secularism. On the contrary, *the whole thing is religious*, religious from one end to the other, inasmuch as "the Force" is a religious or mystical structure and everything in *Stars Wars* is keyed to the Force. The war in *Star Wars* is a religious war, the war of good and evil, between the Republic and the Empire. But the essential point is that the Force is also a *scientific* structure, so that the whole thing is also thoroughly scientific. The religion of *Star Wars* is not at odds with the science of *Star Wars*. There is no dualistic opposition of religion and science, no trace of the war between Galileo and the Church, and certainly no wall of separation between religion and the state. The Jedi Council, composed of twelve members, a biblical number (the twelve tribes of Israel, the twelve apostles), which meets in the Jedi "Temple," is at the political center of the galaxies. Neither is there a dualistic opposition of body and soul, earth and heaven, this life and the next. The old Platonic dualism of matter and spirit adopted in varying degrees by Christian theology has simply been dissolved in the Force. The metaphysics of *Star Wars* is monistic, but not because it is reductionistic or naturalistic. It does not turn everyone and everything into programmable functions of their atomic and subatomic make-up, and it is nothing like the old positivist dream (nightmare) of matter-in-motion determinism, of being able to predict every future state of the universe if you knew the location and velocity of all its parts in any given state and all the laws of physics. On the contrary, situated at the heart of the world of *Star Wars*, the Force is a mystico-religio-scientific structure that gives life mystery and unpredictability and provides a setting for the human drama. For everything depends upon how human beings cooperate with the Force. The Force is the subject of both science and mysticism, and it requires a spiritual discipline and a long preparation to become adept at its ways. The structure of the Force undermines the distinction between theism and atheism.

Things do not divide up that way in *Star Wars*: some people do and some people do not "believe in" the Force, but the Force itself is not an object of "revelation" or of "supernatural faith" as opposed to reason, but a matter of wisdom. The "fool" says in his heart that there is no Force, like the intergalactic junk dealer and gambler Watto, who dismisses the Force as "mind tricks." But the relevant and salient distinction is not between theists and atheists, believers and infidels, but between those who are wise and unselfish enough to work with the Force in harmony and for the rule of justice, and those whose egoist passions distort the Force, creating evil and imbalance in the Force.

The result is that the classic dualisms of Western metaphysics are resolved because they are dissolved, the basis that supports them having been simply withdrawn. The old pre-Copernican metaphorics of the "here (earth) below" and the "beyond" or "heaven above" are gone. The analog to "prayer" in *Star Wars* is to withdraw within, recollect your senses, and allow yourself to be gathered up inwardly and thereby gathered to the Force. You do not look "up" to "heaven" for help. The old cosmology of heaven above, hell below, and earth in the middle that was the self-evident presupposition of the religious imagination of the pre-Copernican world of the Bible is totally absent, having been replaced by a thoroughly contemporary astronomy. Far from putting Galileo under house arrest, the Jedi would have looked upon him as a kind of Moses or the apostle Paul. "Prophet was he," said would have Yoda. The religion of *Star Wars* is relieved of the tensions that beset religious people today, who make daily, hourly use of communications satellites while having inherited religious myths forged in a pre-scientific and rural culture.

In the "Gospel according to Lucas" a world is conjured up in which the intractable oppositions that have tormented religious thinkers for centuries are reconciled, and they are reconciled by being undercut. In the Republic, faith and reason, nature and the supernatural, matter and spirit, are cut from the same cloth. Lucas simply devised a world in which such oppositions are unknown and would make no sense. The gifts that the Jedi masters enjoy have a perfectly plausible scientific basis, even if its ways are mysterious: their bodily cells have a heavier than usual concentration of "midi-chlorians." These are microscopic organisms, possessed by everyone and scientifically measurable, that mediate the Force to us and sensitize us to the Force. When Qui-gon Jinn met Anakin, he ran a blood test to determine Anakin's midi-chlorian count and, having learned that Anakin had an exceptionally high concentration (over twenty thousand), decided that he must be the "chosen one." In effect, he ran a blood test for the Messiah, screening for messianic traits! Humans live in a symbiotic relationship with the midi-chlorians. If we learn to quiet our mind, as in traditional Christian and Buddhist monastic practices, we shall hear what the Force is telling us, for the midi-chlorians communicate the "will" of the Force to us. (By prayer and the silencing of the inner voice, we shall learn the will of God for us.)

Accordingly, the virgin birth in The Phantom Menace has both a scientific explanation and also a mysterious religious dimension. In his counterpart to Luke's nativity narrative, Lucas devises a Shmi Skywalker who is favored by the Force, for "the Force was with her" and comes over her in a hi-tech Annunciation. The Force had done great things in her and she did not put herself or her will ahead of the Force, but uttered a great sci-fi fiat ("let it be done") that echoes across the galaxies and meant that she would remain a slave while Anakin was free to follow his destiny. A son was conceived in her womb who would be called the chosen one, a son of the Force, conceived as he was by the power of the Force, that is, by an extraordinary concentration of midi-chlorians. Lucas is drawing on one of the West's most fundamental narratives: "And he [the Angel Gabriel] came to her and said, 'Greetings, favored one! The Lord is with you . . . The Holy Spirit will come upon you and the power of the Most High will overshadow you . . . Then Mary said, 'Here am I, the servant of the Lord, let it be with me according to your word.' Then the angel departed from her" (Luke 1:28, 35, 38). Of course – in *Star Wars* – things did not turn out quite the way everyone hoped and expected, but that is why there was a story to tell that is going to take nine installments, which will make a lot of money.

We do not have to think that Joseph Campbell – Lucas's religious inspiration and someone with a trendy New Age following himself – is Mircea Eliade in order to see that *Star Wars* has a significant religious dimension. Campbell popularized ideas that go back to Carl Jung's theory of "archetypes," of fundamental transcultural structures deeply embedded in the life of our religious unconscious, and Lucas produced a work of spectacular science fiction that proved an apt vehicle for transmitting these ideas. To be sure, there are other examples: there is an interesting "resurrection" of the Redeemer/Messiah theme in *The Matrix*, which is also interesting, as I said, because the "reality" which everyone experiences in that film is the effect of a computer program. *The Sixth Sense* is a lengthy meditation on life after death, a feature-length film that transpires entirely from the point of view of a dead man. And so on. But *Star Wars*, having picked up something with deep roots in our religious unconscious, and possessing as it does a special skill at re-imagining and re-mythologizing fundamentally religious ideas, has a special edge.

But exactly what does all this mean? Does it mean that the traditional confessions conceived in a pre-Copernican world are obsolete? Do we have to go to popular culture to find religion because the traditional churches have become irrelevant? Has traditional belief become unbelievable to anyone who is not willing to crucify his or her intelligence on the cross of fundamentalism? That would be to go too far. The traditional confessions provide a critical mass for religious faith, supplying a structural and institutional embodiment that keeps our religious memories alive, that undertakes a scrupulous and scholarly study of these memories, and that houses our hopes for the future. They provide an organizing and humanizing power in the daily lives of large numbers of people.

Still, I would say that something *else* is also astir *outside* the churches, that something is slipping beyond or outside the boundaries of the traditional faiths, that a certain religion flourishes without these traditional religions, a religion without religion, and that the sense of religious transcendence has begun to assume new and other forms. The traditional faiths contain something that they cannot contain, and there is an unmistakable tendency today to wrest religious phenomena free from the religions, to reproduce the structure of religion outside the traditional faiths and outside the classic oppositions of religion and science, body and soul, this world and the next. *Star Wars* offers many young people today a high-tech religious mythology, a fairly explicit "repetition" or appropriation of elemental religious structures outside the confines of the institutional religious faiths. Religious transcendence is beginning to transcend the traditional religions. If some of this is just New Age nonsense and superstition, *Star Wars* is a fascinating mélange of mysticism and science fiction that bears witness to a strange symbiosis of religion and post-industrial technologies. "The Force be with you" is a hi-tech expression of an ancient aspiration, an ancient faith, a soaring hope, an abiding love. May the Force be with you, for with the Force nothing is impossible. The Force trades on the ancient name of God, with whom nothing is impossible. In the case of *Star Wars*, science, instead of extinguishing the passion for the impossible as so much mumbo-jumbo, is run together with mystical passion in such a way that it is hard to sort out what is science and what is myth, what is scientific imagination and what is religious imagination. The religious sense of life is not extinguished in *Star Wars*, but re-imagined and re-mythologized. It simply sheds its pre-Copernican tropes and the classic metaphysical dualisms in order to assume a new imaginative form.

God is not dead but alive and well, inside and outside the churches. The gods are everywhere, as old Heraclitus said.

Four

Let us take stock of our argument thus far. Before modernity, the invisible world posited by religious faith was thought to be the *really real*, belonging to a higher order of reality than our life on earth, that than which nothing more real can be conceived, as St. Anselm said. By the end of modernity, religious belief was in various ways denounced as *unreal*, "unmasked" as a fantastic, escapist, reactionary superstition, a fiction woven from our unconscious, our weakness, or our guilt, that hard-nosed Newtonians and all too positive positivists were trying to drive out of our heads. Today, at this point that I describe as post-secular or post-modern, the religious sense of life turns on what I am calling the *hyper-real*, by which I mean a reality beyond the real, the *impossible* that eludes modernity's narrow-minded idea of what is possible. The impossible disturbs the reality of the present from within and leaves us hanging on by a prayer.

This return of the religious, if I may call it that, raises another problem which I must now address before I bring my main argument, which has to do with the structure of religion without religion, to a head in the final chapter. I am referring to the problem of the violent return of religion, the return of religious intolerance and even outright violence, in the various fundamentalist movements around the world, which was one of the main things the old Enlightenment was trying to head off.

A good part of the problem with religion is religious people (without them, religion's record would be unblemished). Religious people, the "people of God," the people of the impossible, impassioned by a love that leaves them restless and unhinged, panting like the deer for running streams, as the psalmist says (Ps. 42:1), are impossible people. In every sense of the word. If, on any given day, you go into the worst neighborhoods of the inner cities of most large urban centers, the people you will find there serving the poor and needy, expending their lives and considerable talents attending to the least among us, will almost certainly be religious people – evangelicals and Pentecostalists, social workers with deeply held religious convictions, Christian, Jewish, and Islamic, men and women, priests and nuns, black and white. They are the better angels of our nature. They are down in the trenches, out on the streets, serving the widow, the orphan, and the stranger, while the critics of religion are sleeping in on Sunday mornings. That is because religious people are lovers; they love God, with whom all things are possible. They are hyper-realists, in love with the impossible, and they will not rest until the impossible happens, which is impossible, so they get very little rest. The philosophers, on the other hand, happen to be away that weekend, staying in a nice hotel, reading unreadable papers on "the other" at each other, which they pass off as their way of serving the wretched of the earth. Then, after proclaiming the death of God, they jet back to their tenured jobs, unless they happen to be on sabbatical leave and are spending the year in Paris.

Religion is for passionate lovers of the impossible, lovers of God, who make the rest of us look like loveless loafers. But at the same time and along with that, these unhinged and impassioned lovers of the impossible are also impossible people who confuse themselves with God and threaten the civil liberties and sometimes even the lives of anyone who disagrees with them, which they take to be equivalent to disagreeing with God. In religion, the love of God is regularly exposed to the danger of being confused with somebody's career, or somebody's ego, or somebody's gender, or somebody's politics, or somebody's ethics, or somebody's favorite metaphysical scheme, to which it is systematically sacrificed. Then, instead of making sacrifices for the love of God, religion is inclined to make a sacrifice of the love of God. That is why we must keep asking day and night, around the clock, "what do I love when I love my God?". Religion, we must always recall, is our doing, not God's, and we should avoid confusing religion or ourselves with God. The religious story of Moses and Aaron is religion's story about itself, where, as a structural matter, religion occupies the place of Aaron and the golden calf, for it can hardly help building man-made idols – buildings and institutions, theologies and hierarchies – which are its stock in trade. We must keep a hammer handy for these idols and be ready to theologize with a hammer – in the name of God. The idea is not to level these structures to the ground, because we need them, the way we need other structures made with human hands, but to keep them open-ended, revisable, honest, on their toes, always threatened and at risk. If, as the Japanese philosopher Kitaro Nishida once said, the religions are rafts that sail on an endless sea, then we must keep watch that we do not allow our preoccupation with the business on the raft to displace God's business, which is love. That is why I have always loved Meister Eckhart's brilliant little prayer, "I pray God to rid me of God," which is a prayer to the ocean of God, whom we love, to rid us of the Gods of the raft.

The situation is quite impossible. Religious people are the people of the impossible, God love them, and impossible people, God help us. Both these things under the same roof, both in the name of God. Like anything else that is worth its salt, religion is at odds with itself, and our job is not to sweep that tension under the rug but to keep it out in the open and allow this tension to be productive.

THE APOSTLE E. F.

The most impossible people of all the people of the impossible, in my view, are the fundamentalists. Fundamentalism is where the tendency to confuse the raft with the ocean, to confuse religion with God, to confuse one's own opinion with God's own Word, to confuse our most low selves with God's Most High glory, can assume its most dangerous form. Religiously speaking, it is a form of idolatry, which has confused God's infinite transcendence with the religious artifacts of human beings. Fundamentalism seems almost impossible for intellectuals to understand. How can we get into the heart or the mind of this strange and provocative phenomenon which looks just plain mad to those of us who fancy ourselves critical and intelligent, or at least post-critical? (Much as I love all these "post-"s, I am not sure I want to be post-intelligent.)

This is a very important question because I do not want to be accused of behaving like an *Aufklärer*, like one more learned despiser of religion, and I do not want to dismiss fundamentalist spirituality as so much nonsense. I want to settle inside this passion for the impossible, to rock with the rhythms of its divine madness, to sway with the joyous pulsations of the Word of God as it shakes the bodily frames and mortal coils of these whole-hearted believers. I want to dance and sing, not sneer!

To get a start on this not inconsiderable task I suggest another trip to the flicks to catch the stunning portrait of one my favorite contemporary film characters, whom I regard as a veritable post-modern St. Paul, an unhinged and impossible lover of the impossible if ever there was one, Euliss "Sonny" Dewey, a.k.a. the Apostle E. F., in Robert Duvall's brilliant 1997 film The Apostle. The film is a penetrating and as I would argue a very Pauline portrait of life deep in the heart of the American "Bible belt," in a dusty little Louisiana town called "Bayou Boutte." While it is sometimes criticized as a vanity vehicle for Duvall's thespian ego, I do not know of a more insightful depiction on film of the religious exaltation, of the religious "enthusiasm" (en-theos, having God within us) that surges through the bodies and souls of people whose whole lives are energized by biblical spirituality. It is hardly an accident that the congregation of the Apostle E. F. (Duvall) is mostly African-American. These Pentecostal Christians sing and dance their hearts out before the Lord in a way that runs together the elemental rhythms and music of African religion with the religion of the Jewish psalmists, producing a magnificent and joyous mania filled with the Holy Spirit, driven by "Holy Ghost power." I am a "Holy Ghost-Jesus-filled preaching machine," E. F. exclaims! Thank you, Jesus! Oui, oui (if I may add a Franco-Cajun touch in honor of contemporary French philosophy!). To no one's surprise, the extras in the film are real people, real preachers and congregations from real churches, gathered together by Duvall – who also wrote, directed, and financed the film, the big studios having been frightened away from doing anything with this much substance.

The Apostle spares us the stupidity of another New Age movie about angels, and the tiresomeness of another film about a charlatan or a con man like Elmer Gantry. In my view, the film belongs to the literature of conversion and invokes the memory of the great conversions of Saul/Paul, the volatile persecutor of the Christians who became Christianity's greatest champion, and of Augustine himself, who, like Duvall's character, also had an eye for women. Unlike Elmer Gantry, Sonny – or the Apostle E. F. (the difference in names is of course significant) – is a sincere man, but he is divided against himself. He is a deeply Pauline figure (the very title of the film intimates this), who can say with the Apostle Paul, one of the models of the character, "I can will what is right, but I cannot do it. For I do not do the good I want, but the evil I do not want is what I do" (Rom. 7: 18–19). By the same token, E. F.'s difficulties also remind us of the "daily war" (bellum quotidianum) with himself that Augustine recounts in the Confessions.

Better at converting others than at converting himself, E. F. swings wildly between love and violence, evangelical passion and jealous rage, a selfless expenditure on apostolic works and explosive anger, preaching God's Word and breaching it. When he invites Jessie, his estranged wife (Farrah Fawcett), to kneel down to pray with him over their break-up, neither she nor we are sure that he does not intend instead to wring her neck for her (not unprovoked) infidelity and for disenfranchising him from his ministry in their Texas home church. He ends up taking a baseball bat and bludgeoning into a coma Horace (Todd Allen), who is Jessie's lover, a youth minister, and their little league coach, after first resisting the temptation to shoot Jessie and Horace dead. He then skips town, assumes his new name, and starts a new life in rural Louisiana, where with engaging evangelical zeal and winning charm he restores an abandoned rural church under the neon banner "One Way Road to Heaven," quickly turning it into an active, vital inter-racial ministry. Still he is not above solidly thrashing a racist troublemaker (Billy Bob Thornton) who appears at his church door one Sunday morning threatening to disrupt service.

A man of God, a man of passion, a man of the Book, for whom the Book is true, down to its smallest parts, its smallest letters, like the letters in the name he assumed when he took flight, E. F. carries the Book with him wherever he goes. He has memorized the canonical sequence of the books of the Old and New Testament, which he can rattle off with dazzling speed. He lays down the Book in front of the giant bulldozer driven up onto the grounds of the church by Billy Bob, who is threatening to level E. F.'s church to the ground in retaliation for the beating he took. The physical presence of the Book stops the giant bulldozer in its tracks, and in a moving scene E. F. sees into Billy Bob's heart, turning his anger and hatred into contrition and reconciliation, turning his heart around, *metanoia*. That conversion scene, a centerpiece of the film and a figure of everything that is at stake in the film, is precisely what Sonny/E. F. must learn to do for himself. He must learn to effect a transformation that will earn him the change of name that signifies the conversion, just as Saul became Paul, and just as Abram became Abraham. In the end, E. F. seems to succeed. He accepts the legal consequences of the assault on Horace and contributes his personal jewelry for the upkeep of the church as the police haul him off to jail – but not without first conducting one rousing, rafter-rocking final service in his church. We last see him in hard labor, leading a prisoner work detail in another stirring song to Jesus – like Paul and

Silas singing hymns to the Lord late into the night in their Macedonian jail (Acts 16: 25).

The transforming passion that surges through the rural church, the rush of "Holy Ghost power," of excitement and exaltation – surely the best portraits on film of such services – is God's passion, unconditioned and uncontained, embracing God's love and God's Word without qualification. If God can take the things that are and make them to be as if they are not (I Cor. 1: 28), one of his parishioners shouts in uncontainable joy, then God can take my troubles and wipe them away and transform me. An excellent bit of scriptural theology! But for Sonny/E. F., happy and unhappy man that he is (Rom. 7:24), that unqualified passion is at once his great strength and his weakness and it is not unrelated to his wild and volatile swings between evangelical ardor and seething anger.

Over and above the Pauline struggle that he wages with himself, what I would single out about E. F. is that he moves about in a world of absolutes, without the human shadings of greys, the twilight of "maybe" and "maybe not," which make up the ambiguity of our lives. When he acts, he acts unconditionally, with unconditional love, or with uncontrolled rage and self-righteousness. When E. F.'s mind is bent on God's work he is a match for the Apostle Paul himself, but when his love goes astray, he is very dangerous. Most men pose no such threat to their neighbor and can offer no such service to God. I would have you hot or cold, but the lukewarm I will spit from my mouth (Rev. 3:16)! Kierkegaard's pseudonymous Johannes Climacus would have no cause to accuse Sonny/E. F. of being a "mediocre fellow."

The "Word of God" is sharper than any two-edged sword indeed (Heb. 4:12): it cuts through the joints and marrow of our vanity and self-will, even as it provides us with a sword of self-righteousness with which to smite our enemies. The cutting edge of the sword, in my view, is its "unconditionality," the sense that we have here been handed an absolute instrument and thereby lifted above the flux of time and the shifting sands of ambiguity, indulging the illusion that God has whispered the Absolute Secret in our ear. Then we feel ourselves absolved from the hard work of sorting out what is human and what is divine in the Scriptures, what is from God and what is just from our ego. The Scriptures are a complex of conflicting messages and we must assume responsibility ourselves for having accepted them as the Word of God, in the first place, and for what we ourselves subsequently make of them. We must do so without laying claim to divine authorization for what is inescapably our own responsibility and our own reading.

After all, whatever else you think of mystics, it is more consistent for a mystic to claim to have been visited in the night by a wordless vision of the Heart of Truth (the trouble starts when the mystics open their mouths, or take pen to paper, which they invariably do!) than for someone to claim that the absolute takes the form of a *book*. For a book is something spelled out in words and letters, which is why theoreticians nowadays prefer to speak of a "text." By speaking of a text they mean to de-emphasize the reassuring unity and engaging authority of the "author" of a "book" and to accentuate the disconcerting effect of working with a woven product, from *texere*, to weave, to string together. For the written work is something interwoven, a bewildering web and complex fabric, sometimes the work of many different authors over the course of very different times stitched together into the illusory and comforting unity of the "book." That textual character is preeminently true of the

Scriptures, whose original context and authorial intention it is impossible to reconstruct with certainty, whose polyphony is the product of layer upon layer of authorship from very different communities and times, which are impossible to unravel. A text admits of endless decontextualization and recontextualization, endless reading and rereading – which is, of course its strength and weakness – and hence of multiple interpretations. When someone who has studied a text for a long time pounds on the table and exclaims, "this is it, this is what it *means*," then we can be sure *not* that they have found what it means in some once and for all final way, but rather that they have finally settled upon their interpretation. A text is just about the *last* thing one should choose if one is in search of an "absolute" instead of an interpretation. That is what all the contemporary fuss about this fuzzy word "hermeneutics" is all about.

Although there is little sign of this in biblical spirituality, "the Bible" – as if that were one just one thing, just one Book, with just one Divine Author – is another case, indeed a paradigmatic case, of the ambiguity and undecidability in things. The absolute love of God is separated from absolute rage by the thin line of the absolute itself, of the illusion of trading in absolutes. Instead of trying to move about in the inhuman and unlivable sphere of unconditional truth and absolute righteousness, we ought to settle for the fallible constructions, construals, and interpretations of a thoroughly mortal and conditioned life, from whose limits we are not relieved even when we say that this is the Word of God and we kiss the Book. Absent that admission, God and death-dealing, religion and violence, will never be far apart.

The Apostle is a rare and insightful film which provides an extraordinary glimpse into the struggles of a religious heart which rocks to the rhythms of biblical spirituality, and that makes it valuable for my purposes. But it is a limited look into the privacy of the heart that steers clear of politics and hence avoids even bigger problems. It never mentions volatile issues like the "right to life," "family values," or teaching evolution in the public schools, the issues that have transformed this lush and living biblical faith into a potent political force. It does not address the question of what happens when such faith goes public, when this joyous biblical spirituality takes a public stand on national issues in a way that has shaken bodies politic around the world. That is the ultimate problem that religious "fundamentalism" poses today, where the conflicting passions that stirred within E. F.'s heart are translated into political action and lead to violence.

FUNDAMENTALISM

Let us start by seeing things from the fundamentalist perspective. The "world," the present age, the *saeculum*, seems quite mad to the fundamentalist mind. To a spirit nourished and cultivated by scriptural images, the late high-tech capitalist democracies look like the biblical Sodom and Gomorrah. For one thing, "sodomy" itself – implying a not so honorable honorary citizenship in an infamous biblical city – is openly defended today as a practice that is no one's business but that of the consenting partners. Homosexuality has come so far out of the closet in which it had been kept by a (hitherto and fading fast) puritanical culture that "domestic partners," or "same-sex marriage" partners, openly sue for legal standing and health benefits. The "traditional family" – increasingly a statistical minority – is weakened by staggering divorce rates and unsettled further by women who refuse to stay home and confine themselves to their traditional role of childbearing and rearing. More and more children are born to unwedded teenagers, to parents addicted to drugs or dying of AIDS, even as millions of unborn fetuses – the numbers should make any sensible person tremble – have had their prospect for life cut off in the bloodiest form of birth control the world has known.

What others might regard as a salutary "pluralism," the "right to choose," and the "right to be different" seems to the ultra-conservative mind a "moral meltdown," an "anything goes" nihilism where nothing is sacred and no one really believes anything. Abortions are protected by law while God and prayer are banned from public places. The "powers and principalities" of the "world," the biblical opposite of the "Kingdom of God," this polymorphic cloth of life at the turn of the millennium, must look as inverted, as mad, as poly-theistic, as idolatrous and corrupt to the ultra-conservative religious mind as the Roman emperors looked to the Jews of the first century. So when, in the midst of this chaos, AIDS, a plague of biblical proportions, descended upon a primarily homosexual population (never mind the many thousands of "straight" people contaminated in blood transfusions), it looks to these ultra-conservatives like the wrath of God being visited upon these proud and disobedient modern-day Sodomites.

Faced with a new Babylon, or a new Sodom, the funda-mentalists clench their fists around the Word of God, which seems to them the one constant in a world gone mad, their one anchor, to which they cling with fierce literalism. The crazier the quilt of the world, the more tenaciously they clutch the letter and the more tightly they draw the net of a literalist religion. The more pluralist and iconoclastic the world gets, the more willing they are to excommunicate from their midst those who do not toe the line on visible and touchstone issues like the subordinate place of women in society, the condemnation of homosexual practices, and abortion. The more decadent the world, the more the sacred remnant of the house of God must preserve its purity. To be sure, these are people with sex on their mind, not social justice, with a passion for sexual purity, not a passion for the poor. The morals that are melting down for them are sexual, not social. They do not burn with passion for immigrants, for the poorest and least among us in our inner cities, or for campaign finance reform (since they are among the biggest spenders when it comes to buying politicians). They do not see the victims of AIDS as the new lepers, with whom Jesus freely mixed and sometimes cured, but as objects of a biblical retribution.

Spurred by a new breed of politically minded leaders, the fundamentalists have gone public and changed the face not only of American politics but of politics around the world. In the United States, fundamentalism is a Protestant phenomenon that has traditionally been antagonistic to Catholicism. The Catholics think that the meaning of the New Testament is its history and tradition, while the fundamentalists think that Catholicism is a history of inventing non-evangelical idols. But in the last two decades we have seen a parallel push toward conservativism in Catholicism and an unprecedented if uneasy alliance of the two religious bodies which has produced a formidable political right wing that has enjoyed a political success that first-generation Barry Goldwater conservatives dared not dream of in the 1960s. The cultural advances that pluralism, secularism, feminism, and the gay and lesbian revolution have made in the past quarter of a century have provided the platform for a highly authoritarian pope, John Paul II, to prosper. Installed in the single most powerful religious office in the world, he waged an epic battle with the "Evil Empire," Eastern European communism, and more than anyone else fired the overthrow of communism in Poland which then spread out from Poland to the other Soviet-bloc states like a mushrooming cloud. Buoyed by such an historic victory against communism, he has been able to direct an iron-fisted crackdown on liberation theologians in South America, to oppose absolutely the recognition of gay and lesbian rights in the church, to block a married priest-hood and the ordination of women. While he is progressive on many social issues – he speaks out against capital punish-ment, condemns Western materialism, and has recently prayed at the weeping wall for forgiveness of Christian anti-Semitism – his agenda in the church, particularly in sexual matters and matters affecting women, is deeply reactionary. That is why prosperous American Roman Catholics, the grandchildren of destitute European immigrants who had joined the Democratic Party in the first half of the twentieth century, joined forces with social conservatives and funda-mentalists in an unprecedented coalition under the common banner of the war on abortion. Together they elected Ronald Reagan and ushered in a conservative and even reactionary period in American politics, under which God's poor have been left even further behind while the wealthiest enjoy unprecedented prosperity.

In the Middle East, the stakes are higher and therefore the violence is even worse, for there an entire culture is at stake. The wave of Islamic revolutions that began with the over-throw of the Shah of Iran and the demonizing of the United States (the great Satan, which helped overthrow a democratic-ally elected government in order to install the anti-communist

Shah) represents a revolution that is at once political, religious, and cultural. Islamic fundamentalists live in a world which is relentlessly invaded by Western technology and communication systems, in which the English language is becoming the *lingua franca*, where the world is becoming a "global market," which means one large *American* market. Western dress, music, films, television, food, and life-styles are everywhere, and with the advent of the internet that trend will become still more ubiquitous and irresistible, with the result that everything distinctively non-Western, everything Arabic and Islamic, is in danger of being washed away. In addition, the Islamic states find themselves up against a state of Israel armed to the teeth with Western munitions, for which they are no military match. With so much at stake, the Islamic upsurge has been swift, severe, and bloody. It is marked by blood-curdling and literalist mutilations (cutting off the hands of thieves, castrating rapists, etc.), stoning criminals to death, an international "contract" or death sentence on Salmon Rushdie for a perceived insult, and severe constraints on women. The greater the perceived need for purity, the bloodier the violence. (The 2000 election results indicate that the people of Iran have become impatient with the rule of the mullahs, but change will have to be gradual if it is to succeed.) Islamic violence is matched on the other side by the unspeakable harshness of life imposed upon the Palestinians by the Israelis, who can no longer claim the moral high ground in their struggle for a homeland. The Palestinians have risen up in righteous indignation against a ruthless oppression held in place by the ultraconservative religious right in Israel, which continues to exercise a crucial swing vote in the Israeli government.

To some extent, fundamentalism is a reaction, not simply

to cultural pluralism, but to the high-tech world which threatens to destroy the stable communities and ancient traditions in which religion has traditionally flourished. But that is too simple. For the various fundamentalisms, Christian, Jewish, and Islamic, have not simply reacted against the high-tech world of advanced post-industrial capitalism and withdrawn into themselves; they have also embraced this world, thus provoking an unstable sympathetic antipathy that is bound to explode. Instead of withdrawing from a world that must seem very alien to their faith, they have entered into an alliance with it that has had an enormous public and especially political impact. Fundamentalism has transplanted the advanced communications systems into its own body and, in order to tolerate the transplant, has suppressed its natural autoimmune systems, as philosopher Jacques Derrida argues. The pope is a jet-age media master, who could give any American political campaign manager a lesson in how to manipulate his image. Protestant "televangelists" bounce signals off satellites circling the earth to preach the Word which some of them actually think implies that the world was created in six days. Islamic terrorists make sure that CNN gets a good camera angle so that the airplane hi-jacking can be broadcast around the globe. Fundamentalists use the latest techniques in media advertising to raise money in order to spread the word that carbon dating is a ruse, that the world is six thousand years old (the liberals will grant that it might be up to eighty thousand years old), that we are all descended from Adam and Eve, that the variety of natural languages is the issue of Babel, and that political candidates who oppose the religious right are agents of Satan.

Fundamentalists establish Christian websites, undertake television ministries to denounce feminists, and set up radio stations featuring call-in talk shows to excoriate feminists, homosexuals, academics, New York City – whoever does not fit into their tiny little xenophobic world. But that alliance with the powers and principalities of this world produces a kind of tic or auto-immune reaction which is the violence that is endemic to fundamentalism. In the United States, abortion clinics are bombed and physicians killed in the name of life and saving the unborn, while terrorist atrocities in the name of God abound in Northern Ireland and the Middle East. That contradiction, murdering and maiming in the name of the right to life, killing in the name of the love of God, is an emblem of the contradiction in which fundamentalists and the radical religious right are caught up today, forced as they are to fall back upon the resources of a world whose basic scientific and cultural presuppositions they reject. They are forced to take nourishment from the fruit of a poisoned tree.

An impossible situation. Fundamentalism is the passion for God gone mad, a way to turn the name of God into the name of terror. The extremism to which fundamentalist religion seems congenitally disposed is, I think, a return of the repressed, to speak psychoanalytically, a reaction to its attempted contraction of the uncontainable love of God – "*everyone* who loves is born of God and knows God" (I John 4:7) – to the constraints of its own narrow culture. Fundamentalism is an attempt to shrink the love of God down to a determinate set of beliefs and practices, to make an idol of something woven from the cloth of contingency, to treat with ahistorical validity something made in time, one more case of Aaron and the golden calf, one more confusion of the raft with the ocean. It represents a failure of religious nerve, a failure to see that the love of God is uncontainable and can assume uncountable and unaccountably different forms.

Fundamentalism attempts to close down the open-ended question "what do I love when I love my God?" with a fixed Answer, to trap the passion for God within literal formulations, to bind up the feet of faith into a finite form instead of allowing it to open upon an infinite abyss. Fundamentalism attempts to repress the abyss within, and the extremism and violence to which it is prone are symptomatic expressions of this repression. It is healthier and less traumatic just to recognize this abyss and to recognize that we are all in this together.

For we do not know what we love when we love our God.

Five

In this final chapter I want to bring my argument to a head. Human experience, I am contending, comes alive as experience by and through the impossible. Experience is really experience, something that really happens, something to write (home) about, only when we are pushed to the limit of the possible, to the edge of the impossible, driven to an extreme, which forces us to be at our best. Now since this experience of the impossible is the very quality that also defines religion for me, then I am arguing that there is a fundamentally religious quality to human experience itself, whether or not you have the blessings of the bishop or the rabbi, whether or not you subscribe to one of the institutional faiths at all, whether or not you believe in the "God" of one of the traditional confessions, whether or not you are an "atheist" vis-à-vis the several theisms. There is a deeply religious element within us all, with or without religion, so this little essay on religion is also an essay on being human. That is how I gloss the talk of a "religion without religion" that I have borrowed from philosopher Jacques Derrida, and it is by defending that idea head on that I wish to conclude this study.

RELIGIOUS TRUTH/TRUE RELIGION

I am inching toward another idea of "religious truth," which is a centerpiece of my little treatise *On Religion* (*Without Religion*).

The idea is to move beyond literalism, fundamentalism, and outright superstition without simply repeating an Enlightenment critique of religion whose presuppositions, as I have argued, have been widely discredited. For a religion without religion requires a full charge of "religious truth" where that is to be sharply distinguished from "true religion" in the sense of "the one true religion" (by which we always mean, invariably, mine-not-yours). The several religions, in the plural, are unique and irreducible repositories of their distinctive ethical practices and religious narratives, representing so many different ways to love God, but without laying claim to an exclusive possession of "The Truth." In the Confessions Augustine said that the Scriptures may have many meanings, so long as all of them are true. That I would say also goes for religion. We may and need to have many religions, and many "sacred scriptures," so long as all of them are true.

Any given religion is better off without the idea that it is "the one true religion" and the others are not, as if the several religions were engaged in a zero sum contest for religious truth. They need to drop the idea of "the true religion," to stop running "negative ads" about everyone else's religion or lack of religion, and to kick the habit of claiming that their particular body of beliefs is a better fit with what is "out there," as if a religion were like a scientific hypothesis, which is the mistake of the Creationist "scientists." Unlike a scientific theory, there is not a reason on earth (or in heaven) why many different religious narratives cannot all be true. "The one true religion" in that sense makes no more sense than "the one true language" or the "one true poetry," "the one true story" or "the one true culture." While rejecting the modernist idea that science is the exclusive depository of truth, we should have learned something from modernity –

post-modern means having passed through and learned a thing or two from modernity – namely, that religious truth is true with a truth that is of a different sort than scientific truth. Religious truth is tied up with being truly religious, truly loving God, loving God in spirit and in truth (John 4:24), and there are more ways to do that than are dreamt of by the faithful in the traditional confessions. Loving God in spirit and in truth is not like having the right scientific theory that covers all the facts and makes all the alternative explanations look bad.

The faithful need to concede that they do not cognitively *know* what they *believe* by faith in any epistemologically rigorous way. While faith gives the faithful a way to view things, they are not lifted by the hook of faith above the fray of conflicting points of view. They do not enjoy certain cognitive privileges and epistemic advantages of which others have been deprived, and their beliefs are not entitled to special treatment outside their own communities (which I encourage them to maintain and promote, with all of the tensions that beset community life). To be sure, a religion without religion cannot do without religious truth. There is indeed something deeply true about religion, but it is, I claim, *a truth without knowledge*, by which I mean without absolute or capitalized Knowledge, without laying claim to enjoying privileged cognitive, epistemic, propositional information that has been withheld from others. "Knowledge puffs up," St. Paul said, "but loves builds up. Anyone who claims to know something does not yet have the necessary knowledge; but anyone who loves God is known by Him" (I Cor. 8: 1–2). Love trumps knowledge and knowledge is at its best when it concedes what it does not know, whereas loving can never brag about not loving. Any given faith is certainly a way to see and to know, one more among many, since indeed all genuine knowing is knowing "as," and all knowledge depends upon faith, and all faith is a way of seeing, construing, knowing. But faith lacks the wherewithal to absolutize its perspective, to lift itself up above the others in Capitalized form and cow the rest of us into submission. The faithful need to concede that their faith is the historical shape that the love of God has assumed for them, the historical way they have been gifted to see things, and that it is "true" in the same way that a novel can be deeply "true" even though it is rightly classified as "fiction," not "fact." There are many ways to know and love God: "*everyone* who loves is born of God and knows God" (I John 4:7), too many to contain or to count. The several religious communities thus need to remember that "hospitality" requires them to sharpen their sense of the historical contingency of their language, symbols, and formulations, the contingency of the setting of their faith in a particular place and time, in a particular tradition. The faithful need to remind themselves that "others" – people who have never heard of the "God of Israel," "Allah," "the name of Jesus," or any of the long-forgotten names of God in languages of which we no longer retain a trace, not to mention the inhabitants of distant galaxies, which is a post-Ptolemaic consideration – do not share and *cannot be expected* to share their "confessional faith," their favorite body of approved propositions, any more than the faithful can be expected to share the approved propositional faith of others. Religious truth, the love of God, does not have to do with approved propositions.

The idea of a religion without religion amounts to the recommendation that we return to the medieval sense of *vera religio*, where "religion" meant a virtue, not a body with institutional headquarters in Nashville or the Vatican, so that "true religion" meant the "virtue" of being genuinely or truly religious, of genuinely or truly loving God, not The One True Religion, Ours-versus-yours. God is more important than religion, as the ocean is more important than the raft, the latter bearing all the marks of being constituted by human beings. Religion, which is a human practice, is always deconstructible in the light of the love of God, which is not deconstructible. We need to spare ourselves from the extremism and madness that are involved when the faithful get it into their heads that "we" – Jews or Christians, Hindus or Muslims, whoever – have been granted a privileged access to God in a way that has been denied to others, or that we are loved by God in special way that God just cannot bring "himself" (sic!) to feel for others, or that we have been given certain advantages that God just has not granted others. Notice that "*we*" – this is just about what we mean by "we" – never imagine that God revealed himself to and loves someone *else* in a privileged way and that we are a third party to this intimate relationship between God and his beloved and will have to settle for second best, looking in from the outside, our noses pressed hard against the glass of their religion. We need to steer around the dangerous path of imagining that God plays favorites, that God favors or has "chosen" Jews but not Egyptians, or Christians but not Muslims, that in general God has revealed Himself to "us," but not to the "others," to Paul on the way to Damascus but not to the rest of the Jews who stuck with the Torah, that God prefers men to women in order to do "His" work, or white people to black, or Western Europeans to Asians, or has in some way or other granted special privileges to a particular individual or nation, race or gender – or planet or galaxy! – in a particular time and language, that has been withheld from others.

It is always possible – in fact, you can bet on it – that someone might fold their hands and piously looking up to heaven tell us that we must take the bull by the horns and face up to the fact that God's special revelation at just one time and place to just one people in just one language is all part of a Great Divine Mystery, that God's ways are not our ways. *Excuse me?* There is nothing divine or mysterious about that (although there is a great deal of bull). It sounds much more like our ways, not God's, our own very unmysterious and human all too human ethnocentrism and egocentrism, our own nationalism and narcissism, our own sexism, racism, and self-love writ large, in short, a gross human weakness that is being passed off as a Great Divine Attribute. The *nerve* of some people! The exclusivist claim that almighty God has been *exclusively* revealed to a particular people, at a particular time, in a particular place and language, is at the root of a good deal of the violence that religion perpetrates in the name of God, whose name is supposed to be love, not war. There are many ways for God to be revealed, too many to contain in a book entitled *On Religion*, too many to be contained within the limits of our historical and cultural imaginations, and many, many ways for religions to be true, too many to count. True religion, genuine religiousness, means loving God, which means a restlessness with the real that involves risking your neck; it means serving the widow, the orphan, and the stranger in the worst streets of the most dangerous neighborhoods, *without* getting trapped by the claim to a privileged divine revelation made by the particular religions. "God is love, and those who abide in love abide in God, and God abides in them" (I John 4: 16).

Anyone, anywhere, anytime. Period!

Religious truth is not the truth of propositions, the sort of truth that comes from getting our cognitive ducks in order, from getting our cognitive contents squared up with what is out there in the world, so that if we say "S is p" that means that we have picked out an Sp out there that looks just like our proposition. Religious truth belongs to a different order, to the order or sphere of what Augustine called "facere veritatem," "making" or "doing" the truth, even if, especially if, what we are called upon to do exceeds our powers and we are asked to do the impossible. Even if, especially if, we have become unhinged, and have sunk to our knees in faith, hope, and love, praying and weeping like mad. "No one has ever seen God" (I John 4: 12) – that is, when it comes to God, nobody's cognitive ducks are in order. So if we say "God is love," that means that we are expected to get off our haunches and do something, make that truth happen, amidst our sisters and our brothers, not that we have just nailed something in rerum natura, as when we say "the moon is a satellite of the earth." We must say and pray, sing and dance, shout and whisper "God is love" – with all the gusto of E. F.'s "One Way Road to Heaven" congregation, or with all the solemnity of the monks of Gethsemane at morning matins – in spirit and in truth, which means in deed, for the name of God is the name of a deed. We must get something done, or better let it be done (fiat!), let something impossible get done in us. Notwithstanding the objections raised by the logicians (a difficult breed, notoriously hard of heart, with grossly overgrown cognitive and proposition-making faculties), "doing the truth" is not a category mistake. On the contrary, it is the very truth of religious truth, what is true and truthful and honest about religious truth, which is also why we can be very truthful in disclaiming that we have any secret access to The Truth. Religious truth is a truth without Knowledge. Religious truth is a *deed*, not a thought, something that demands our response, without pretense or dissemblance, that costs us our blood and our tears, even if we do not know who we are. Especially then. Otherwise it is a hollow bell, a tinkling cymbal, a lot of noise (I Cor. 13:1) – or a list of propositions drawn up at a conference of well-fed theo-logicians.

The theologians, God bless them, tell us that faith must be "certain," otherwise it is waffling, and what good is that? By "certain" they do not mean transparent, for faith is through a glass darkly, not face to face (I Cor 13:12). They mean that it must be held "securely" by the will which will not let it waver, and even that it can be "testified" to up to the point of death and martyrdom, which is decidedly not waffling. But testimony still does not turn faith into Knowledge, into "seeing God," although it gives faith a quality of "truth" in this sense of *facere veritatem*, which is a certain sort of truth without Knowledge that I am trying to defend. Having faith means testifying (which is what the Greek *martyreo* means) to the love of God, doing something, a deed, making justice flow like water over the land, not getting a proposition right. Nor does testimony lift the love of God up above the historically limited and culturally situated contexts in which it always takes root and finds the words to formulate itself. It is precisely this confusion of religious truth with Knowledge that crosses the fatal line between being willing to die for the love of God and being willing to kill, that emboldens the faithful to wage war in the name of God against everyone who does not share their faith. That is one reason I agree with Paul, who, champion though he was of faith, says that of the three passions for the impossible, love is the greatest (I Cor. 13:13), which means that love is a way to keep faith, which is through a glass darkly, from driving us into a ditch.

God is more important than religion as love is more important than faith. Religions are rafts, human artifacts, historical constructions that are organized in their particulars by human communities in order to articulate the love of God, and their human origins keep showing through their seams. The faithful constantly congratulate themselves with the belief that their religion is "instituted by God," and that is certainly true in the sense that the various religious forms of life arise in *response* to something that has swept us away, something impossible, something other or wholly other to which we are responding, which has driven us to the limit. But human beings are responsible for all the particulars of the response, for the vocabularies, the theologies, and all the institutional structures, which formulate in definite and determinate ways *just what* has swept them away. These are all eminently deconstructible, as any scrupulously close history of any given religion will reveal in painful detail. The faithful rarely have the heart to hear a cold and heartless rendering of the history of the human formation of their religious tradition, which they prefer to believe has dropped from the sky. The only thing I think has dropped from the sky, so to speak, is the love of God, which I have been arguing descends upon us in the form of a question, "what do I love when I love my God?". So what has dropped from the sky is not The Answer with which I may smite my enemies, but a question with which I am myself put in question! God is a question, not an answer, the most radical thought we can entertain, that exposes the questionability of all the other answers we think we have, exposing the fragility of the raft, the revisability of the determinate structures within which the various religions conduct their business, forcing them to ask themselves again and again, "what do I love when I love my God?".

However robust our faith, faith is also unnervingly fragile. The fragility of faith is in part a function of the multiplicity of the formulations of the several faiths, of the multiplicity of religious traditions, each of which represents its own integral and irreducible form of life, each of which is true without Knowledge, which is why I speak of a religion without religion. But that is only part of the story. For beyond the historical particularity and cultural contingency of the forms it assumes, which can also be quite lovely, the love of God is inwardly disturbed by something more distressing, something more stark and unlovely, indeed utterly loveless, which I shall call here, not without a flare, "the tragic sense of life." The love of God is haunted by a specter that causes it to pass many a sleepless night. If Ebenezer Scrooge had his sleep disturbed by three very upsetting ghosts, the advantage he had over me is that he at least knew the names of the ghosts that haunted him, which is perhaps why it all turned out well in the end, and he also got it all over with in one sleepless night. But my problem is that I am permanently spooked by an "anonymous" spirit, by a specter whose name is "no name," "no one," "no-one-knows-we-are-here," a loveless specter who revisits me night after night. For the name of God, and the love of God, always transpires against the background of an anonymous and loveless force in things, which is why I am always asking, "what do I love when I love my God?".

One way to look at religion is to see it as turning on the question, "Does anyone know or care that we are here?" In this world of time and happpenstance, of good fortune and bad, of pleasure and pain, of surpassing joys and nightmarish cruelty and unhappiness, is anyone watching? Does anyone take notice or care? Is there something in things that rises above the flux of the shifting tides of time and fortune to give it all sense? Does God "in heaven" watch over us, counting every tear, numbering every hair on our heads, knowing what is in the heart of each one of us? Is there someone to whom we can pray like mad, like Augustine in the *Confessions* praying and weeping over stolen pears, someone who sees the secrets of our hearts, who weighs the good against the evil, and steers all things mightily and wisely unto good?

Or are we rather, as Nietzsche mused, just so many little animals scurrying across the surface of a little planet in a far-off distant corner of the universe inventing proud words for ourselves – like "the love of God"? In time, Nietzsche says, the little planet will run out of steam and sink back into its sun and be reduced to ash, and the little animals and their noble words will have to die. And what then? The cosmos will simply draw another breath and move on, utterly unmindful of us and uncaring, without regret and without so much as giving us a thought, since it does not think in the first place. Shall we and all our lovely words vanish without a trace? Shall we all have been speaking forgotten languages? Is that our story, our history, our fate? That numbing thought is what I am calling the *tragic* sense of life, and you can see why it keeps me pacing the floors night after night.

Does anyone know we are here? Does anyone care? Are we on our own? Is there nothing beyond the heartless and unrelenting cosmic rhythms, nothing loving, kind, or fair? Should we not, following Nietzsche's advice, simply stiffen our spines, cut the whining, and learn to love this fate, learn to love the flickering moment of time allotted us without asking too many questions, without looking for something more? Should we simply learn to take life straight up, without the admixture of anything to sweeten or attenuate it, to blunt its sharp edge? Should we not take the gift of life for what it is, say "yes" to it for what it is, neither more nor less, without any additions or subtractions? Yes to life. Just as it is? Yes. With all its joys and sorrows, pleasures and pains, births and deaths, kindnesses and cruelties linked together in a single chain, inextricably entangled with each other? Yes, yes. Thus spoke Zarathustra.

The *religious* sense of life, which I have defined as the love of God, takes shape in the face of this facelessness, is forged over and against this tragic sense. To be sure, by a certain accounting, the tragic view is already a kind of religion, a rather phallic religion forged out of tragedy, where the love of God takes the form of saying "yes" to the tragic fate of the god Dionysus, of loving necessity, *amor fati*, which means the loveless love of loving a loveless fate. Then the debate between the tragic and the religious would have to be recast as an intramural dispute transpiring within religion, between a tragic religion and a non-tragic one, between the love of *necessity* and the love of *the impossible*. It might be possible to work things out like that, but I think that in the end that would muddy the waters and take religion and the love of God so loosely that they begin to lose all sense, which will become plain in what follows. I see the love of God as permanently opposed and exposed to this love of loveless anonymity, as haunted and disturbed from within by it. Furthermore, on my impudent hypothesis, which is that we get the best results from facing up to the worst and not putting too sanguine a spin on things, religion should renounce even *trying* to insulate itself from the tragic view. Religion is co-constituted by the tragic sense, which is both the very sense that would undo it and the sense against which it itself takes shape. For the *tragic* keeps the religious honest, keeps it on its toes, and blocks the triumph-alism and self-enclosure of the impossible people I have com-plained about, and brings more sharply into focus what I am calling here a truth without Knowledge.

Let there be no mistake. I am not giving the tragic the last word. I am not saying that after hearing religion's long and lovely discourse on the love of God, the tragic comes along at the last moment and scores a knock-out punch in the last round by exposing the naive and childlike heart of religion, while counseling us all to grow up, for religion is our child-hood and enlightened disillusionment is our maturity. I am not saying that the tragic is the real truth, because I think that the tragic view is also just one more perspective, just another take on things. The problem is that, like any ghost worth its salt, I cannot make it go away; it haunts me day and night. But haunting though it be, it is a little too romantic and a little too macho to steal my heart. There is something perversely *appeal-ing* about the tragic view, a certain heroic hopelessness, a phal-lic fist-shaking defiance that enjoys cursing the darkness and even dances to the tune, that says "yes" to it, that goes chin to chin with the cosmos and dares it to break our will. Let us love life, this phallic romanticism says, for life is cruel but it is innocent of wrong-doing and we are tough as nails. What does not kill me, Nietzsche crowed, makes me stronger, hap-pier, healthier, more sublime – yes, yes! That is why I resist calling all this the love of God; it is a little more like loving orgasms (which, I hasten to add, I do not *simply* oppose), or like the braggadocio of the "boys" after a game.

But above all I do not give the final word to this macho heroics precisely on the grounds of my salt-giving criterion of truth, which I have taken from St. Augustine, *facere veritatem*, which is where I think the tragic view comes up short. On the tragic view both the cruel indifference of natural disasters and the malice in the human heart are of a kind, equally *innocent*, equally the outcome of the impersonal and unknowing forces of nature. Are the fierce winds and waves guilty because they destroy the seaside homes of thousands of people and take their lives? Or the rains that flood the streets and towns and farmlands? Or the hawk that sweeps down upon its prey? Or the lion that preys upon the fawn? (So far, so good, but let's go on.) Or the Nazi executioners who "exterminated" millions of "innocent" people in the name of a hideous ideology? Or the terrorists who maim the bodies and take the lives of "innocent" children? You see the snag, the hook on which we are hung by tragic phallo-logic? If everything is innocent, innocent children have no special claims as against the equally innocent forces that slaughter them for personal profit, greed, and self-aggrandizement. There is no moral difference between a foul wind and a cigarette manufacturer out to make a profit by hooking vulnerable youngsters on carcinogens. The whole bloody thing is just the way the bloody cosmic forces play themselves out. You cannot separate the doer from the deed, the forces from the way the forces discharge themselves. You might be able to say that some forces produce great works of art or lasting institutions, and that these are "higher" or more "powerful" forces, and that those that engage in genocide are "lower" and "meaner," but that would be a purely "aesthetic" way to look at things. And it would also be fatalistic – how could *amor fati* not be? – inasmuch as there is no suggestion here that anyone could *do* otherwise. For we are as we are and we do what we do, just the way it is only a fiction of grammar to think that there is a distinguishable "it" that does the deed when we say "it rains." That is why this tragic line fails the test of the *facere veritatem* and why, by the way, the *lovers of the necessary* are usually tied up with right-wing politics; they usually tell us to have the steel to love things the way they are, and not to coddle the weak or the poor, while religious people, who are *lovers of the impossible*, are down in the bad neighborhoods trying to change things, *doing the truth*. For the religious sense of life, the bonds of the present are not nailed down by necessity but broken open by the possible, by the possibility of the impossible.

The religious relationship to the world arises in the face of this facelessness and hopelessness, which is why no less a critic of religion than Karl Marx said that religion is the heart of a heartless world. The great religious symbols and figures have always been figures of suffering, for the love of God always comes to rest upon the least among us, upon the ones who suffer needlessly. If anyone is indeed "privileged" by God, it is the underprivileged, because with God the last are first. The name of God is the name of the One who takes a stand with those who suffer, who expresses a divine solidarity with suffering, the One who says *no* to suffering, to unjust or unwarranted suffering. Thus the defining moment of Jewish history is the Exodus, the escape from slavery, so that the name of God is the name of the liberator, the One who leads the Jews out of Egypt. In Christianity the central symbol is the "Crucifixion," a slow, sadistic, hideous, and torturous execution used by the Romans to put some teeth in the *"pax" Romana*, which any court today would readily declare a cruel and inhuman punishment. The Crucifixion has been portrayed by so many beautiful works of art, and reproduced as exquisite gold and diamond-studded jewelry worn by opulently adorned clerics, people who make a profitable living off the Crucifixion, as Kierkegaard said, that we quite forget that it is a gallows or a death chamber. Wearing reproductions of it is like dangling miniature diamond-studded gold "electric chairs" around our neck. But the meaning of the Cross is that God chose to manifest solidarity with an innocent man, a convicted criminal, legally speaking, who suffered an ignominious execution, just the way Paul says that God chose to manifest solidarity with the foolish of this world to shame the wise, and with the low-born nobodies (*ta me onta*) to shame those who "are" (I Cor. 1: 28), the powers that "be."

I am arguing for a radical and inescapable fluctuation or "undecidability" between what we have called here the tragic and the religious sense of life. There is no cognitively definitive way to settle what is what or what is going on, no way to adjudicate their dispute, no knock-down argument for the one and against the other. We do not find the religious *without* the tragic, or when you do it is because the tragic has been violently suppressed, repressed, or excluded, which means that we are then threatened by a return of the repressed, which is pretty much how the powerful convulsions of fundamentalist violence are to be interpreted, as I argued above. At the core of fundamentalism, I maintain, there lies a repressed fear that faith is only faith and as such a risk with no guarantee of anything, which is the truth about religion to which it testifies in the mode of repressing it. The religious sense of life grows up in the face of this facelessness, against its backdrop. The anonymity is inexpungeable; it is first, last, and constant, preceding and following faith, all the while invading the very interstices of our faith.

For however much the several religious faiths flourish, we must all "fess up" that we do not know who we are or what is going on, not "Really," not in some "Deep Way," although we all have our views. No one really knows what they love when they love (their) God, even if they do not lack for words when we ask them. That indeed is the condition of their faith, the reason their faith is faith, not Knowledge, and why religion can be true without Knowledge, why religion is also without religion. Faith is faith in the face of the facelessness of the anonymous. Faith is always haunted and disturbed from within by this specter of a heartless world of cosmic forces, where the waves that beat against the shore and the murderous hearts of violent men and violent regimes are all part of the cosmic economy, all part of the way the forces discharge themselves, all part of the cosmic ebb and flow, where many an innocent lamb is sacrificed on the altar of the cosmic play. Faith is faith that there is something that lifts us above the blind force of things, a mind in all this mindlessness. That there is something – like the Force in Star Wars, which is, as we have seen, a bit of a transcription of the Buddha nature – or someone, as in the personal conceptions of God found in the great monotheisms, who stands by us when we are up against the worst, who stands by others, by the least among us. Faith is faith that we can say that certain things are wrong, are evil. Faith is the memory of evil done, the dangerous memory of suffering that cannot be undone, and the hope of a transforming future.

THE FAITH OF A POST-MODERN

I am slowly working my way back to my beginning, that religion is the love of God. "God is love," which is my religious centerpiece, cuts both ways. It could mean what Augustine means, that when we love anything, it is really God whom we love, however obscurely. Or it could mean what French feminist philosopher Luce Irigaray means, that love is a divine force, a divine milieu that sweeps the lovers up into each other's arms and allows them to embrace and intermingle with each other. Then the name of God is one of the names we have for love, one of the oldest and most prestigious names, to be sure, maybe even a *primum inter pares*, but still just one of many names, and what we *really* mean by "God" is *love*. There is a certain undecidability here, by which I mean an inability to put a stop to the translatability or substitutability of these two terms, "God" and "love." The love of God – or the god of Love? How are we to tell which is really a translation of which, which is a substitute for which? How can we resolve this fluctuation, decide this undecidability?

The troublemaker here is the word "*really*," which is attempting to "unmask" the passion for love as a passion for God, or, alternately, to "unmask" the passion for God as a passion for love. The first unmasking is pre-modern, theological, and uplifting, always looking up to the sun to explain the patches of light here below. The latter unmasking is modernist, critical, and desublimating, belonging to the spirit of an age of a secularizing reason which tries to cut religious figures down to size, to fit them within the limits of reason alone, or explain them away altogether. Either way, the unmasking claims to boil things down to the way they *really are*, to provide the final word about what is *really real*, to settle the matter once and for all, to decide things one way or the other. But one of the things that the word "post-modern" would have meant had it been able to hold on and mean something relatively determinate (which, alas, seems not to have happened) is the *end* of all those projects of unmasking and of cutting through to what is Really Real, the renunciation of the attempt to speak the Final Word, be that a sublimating Theological Final Word or a desublimating Critical Final Word. One of the things "post-modern" would have meant is de-capitalization, the willingness to get along as best we can without capital letters and without final authoritative pronouncements, without a Knowledge of the Secret, and to splash about in the waters of undecidability.

For we do not know who we are.

What then? Comes the chaos? Does all hell break loose? Are we left without any guidance? If we do not know who we are, or what we love, what is left for us?

We are not left with nothing, but with the passion and the not-knowing. The passion of not knowing, truth without Knowledge, the restless heart. *Inquietum est cor nostrum*. We are not left for dead, as some would think, who require a firm foundation, an absolute propositional base, before taking a single step forward, or left to drift aimlessly, bobbing on the surface of an endless sea. We are left a little lost, no doubt about that – *quaestio mihi factus sum*, Augustine said, but, to stay with the marine metaphor, swimming like hell (holy hell, to be sure), *facere veritatem*, doing the truth with all the passion of non-knowing, asking all the more insistently, "what do I love when I love my God?". But the whole idea behind this argument for a post-secular position is to avoid being drawn into the fray about what is really real and to make a leap of love into the *hyper-real*, to the real beyond or up ahead, which eye hath not seen or ear heard. There is, I am arguing, a kind of endless translatability or substitutability, a holy undecidability, let us say, between God and love, or God and beauty, or God and truth, or God and justice, in virtue of which we cannot resolve the issue of which is a version of which, which is the translation of which, which is the substitute for which. Not if we are *honest*. But by insisting on "honesty," I am saying of course that if the truth be told, we *really* do not know. But is that not a fatal, performative contradiction (which is how professional philosophers say "Gotcha!" in their journals), my own gesture of unmasking? Am I not hoisted on my own petard, snagged on the very hook of the "really" to which I have just said we should show the door? Not so, I would say (not really). I am not trying to unmask both positions, to trump both of them by means of a third, still higher, triumphant and triumphal unmasking than which there is no greater unmasking. I am just trying to swear off unmasking and concede that I really do not know which is which. I am not trying to excommunicate the word "really" from our vocabulary, which I really could not do anyway, but only to say that I really do not know what is Really Real, and that I have pledged my troth to the hyper-real, to making the impossible happen. Undecidability is the place in which faith takes place, the night in which faith is conceived, for night is its element. Undecidability is the reason that faith is faith and not Knowledge and the way that faith can be true without Knowledge. It is when we recognize that we do not know who we are, or what is *really* going on, despite our several takes on it, that faith and hope and love are called for, and the time has come to give our heart to the hyper-real.

I am simply saying, or confessing, in a kind of post-modern Augustinian confession, that we do not know who we are – to which I hasten to add: and *that* is who we are. We are not thereby left with nothing but rather with ourselves, with the *quaestio mihi factus sum*. We are left holding the bag – of our *passion*, the passion of our non-knowing, our passion for God, of our love of God, where we do not know what we love when we love our God. A good many religious people think that passion must be fixed and determinate and nailed down, that a passion must have a definite destination. They think that a passion must keep its head and know where it is headed, and they are scandalized by the very idea of a passion of non-knowing. I have nothing against passions that know where they are heading, and I do not deny that they have their place, but I do not think that is the deepest or most interesting form of passion. If a passion of non-knowing runs the risk of getting lost, a passion that knows what it is about and has a good idea about how things are going to turn out is in danger of resting on its oars and becoming a mediocre fellow; it risks becoming a routinized and rote performance, which is putting in its time until the end result rolls around. In my view, the very highest passion is driven by non-knowing. Its tensions are heightened and the stakes are raised when we lack assurance about what is going on, or how things will turn out, when all we can do is push on, have faith, keep going, love and trust the process about which we lack any final assurance. Passion falls back on faith and faith is a kind of passion. Passion is guided by faith and faith is driven by passion, and this passionate faith is what gives life savor and salt.

But if that is so, then, contrary to what a good many ortho-religious people think, people who are rigidly attached to the particular figures and symbols and propositions by which they have been formed, *we do not know what we believe or to whom we are praying.* To be sure, we can all recite our prayers and various creeds, and thanks to the theologians, bless their hearts, we know the propositional contents of what we confess, sometimes in very great detail, sometimes knowing more than we need to know! But these creedal statements are trying to give propositional form to a living faith and a radically different form of truth; they present religious truth sometimes very well and in inspiring forms, and sometimes in certain well-formed, prepackaged, freeze-dried formulations, some of which have been voted on by councils and assemblies of (mostly male) elders. But beneath them, within them, before and after them, stirs a living faith, a restless heart, in love with love. A faith *in what*? A love *of what*? Given what I have been saying about undecidability, about the endless translatability and substitutability of names like "God" and "love," that question must remain open, and as long as it does, as long as it is not answered, as long as it is not closed down, then faith is faith indeed. If we really do not know who we are, then faith is really faith. Undecidability protects faith and prayer from closure and in keeping them thus at risk also keeps them safe.

But if the question of faith resists an answer, a Big, Final Conclusive Answer, it requires a *response*, a modest but passionate, humble but heartfelt response. When faith and love call the roll, we had better answer, like the Virgin Mary in Luke's story, "here I am." When love calls for action, we had better be ready with something more than a well-formed proposition even if it has been approved by a council. We had better be ready with a *deed*, not a *what* but a *how*, ready to respond and do the truth, to make it happen here and now, for love and justice are required now. The love of the not yet real, of the impossible and hyper-real, and the memory of the dead who must not have died in vain, requires a deed, here and now, in spirit and in truth. Religious truth, being truly religious, is not a formula to recite but a deed to do. "Beloved, let us love one another, for love is from God; everyone who loves is born of God and knows God" (I John 4:7). The name of God is something to *do*. Without the *deed*, without doing the love, it is just noise, or a way to get my own way, or to earn a comfortable living for his reverence, or to smite my enemies with a large and massive sword.

Prayer, too, is a form of truth without Knowledge. When a Protestant prays to the crucified Christ, or a Catholic prays for the intercession of the Blessed Virgin or celebrates the Holy Eucharist, or a Buddhist bows humbly before a statue of the Buddha, or when Muslims turn earnestly toward the East and sink to their knees, *who is getting it right?* That question is not only wrong-headed and non-sensical – like seeking the one true language – but it is also impious, irreligious, and insolent, for we have to do here with integral and mutually irreducible forms of life. Each form of prayer is the issue of its own intensity, heartfelt sincerity and humility, its own good will, and makes sense inside the historical form of life that nourishes it. Each represents its own way of doing the truth. We should have many religions and many prayers, so long as all of them are true, so long as all of them are doing the truth. But none of them has absolute or transhistorical credentials. Far from it. Each is nested in a historical setting from which it cannot possibly be extricated without being destroyed. Each is an historical *how*, not a transhistorical *what*. Far from assuring us that we know who we are praying to, their very diversity assures us that while the prayers of the faithful come in many historical forms, we do not know in some overarching ahistorical way to whom we are praying, for prayer can be true without Knowledge. The diverse forms assumed by the life of prayer assure us that the essence of prayer does not turn on resolving that indecision, on determinately nailing down the *what*, but, once again, on "doing the truth," praying in spirit and in truth (John 4:24) – in multiple, irreducibly, disconcertingly different ways. If God is anywhere, it is in the diversity. Augustine also liked to ask, "where are you, O Lord," to which the right answer, the most orthodox of answers, is "everywhere," inside me and outside me, within me and above me, here and over there, for God has pitched his tent and dwells among us and, to add my own post-modern pitch, she dwells among others as well. *Everyone who loves is born of God.*

AXIOMS OF A RELIGION WITHOUT RELIGION

I have been arguing for opening up the lines of communication between the life of faith before modernity and the post-secular moment we are presently experiencing. I have been proffering a post-modern or post-secular repetition of St. Augustine, a reiteration of St. Augustine for a post-secular time, which has all the makings of a religion without religion (upon which Augustine *the bishop* might sometimes cast a disapproving episcopal glance). Accordingly I would like to propose my own *fin de* millennium version of St. Augustine's and St. Bonaventure's *itinerarium mentis ad deum*, a kind of post-modern ascent of the mind to God, or to the impossible, or to the hyper-real. It is designed for people like me, people whom Kierkegaard liked to call "poor existing individuals" (that's me), by which I mean those who do not know who they are. I describe an ascent that unfolds in three phases, which given this Kierkegaardian allusion we might also characterize as three stages of post-modern "existence," or of what I shall call three gradually higher or more radical axioms of a religion without religion.

"I do not know who I am or whether I believe in God." That is a start, and it is true enough. I am a mystery unto myself, a question mark, an enigma, a land of turmoil and difficulty, as Augustine said. Accordingly I fluctuate between faith and faithlessness, God and Godlessness, religion and irreligion, not knowing which one is me or mine, or where I belong. That is true enough, but it is not enough truth, in the sense of the *facere veritatem*, which means that it is too cognitivist and not passionate enough. The fellow peddling this line is too

much inclined to stay home and not venture out at all in bad weather, to go below when foul winds blow, to sit back in his chair and puff on his cigar of a stormy afternoon and let life run its course, wondering how it will all turn out for those poor beggars outside who are caught in life's tempests. Undecidability here runs too close to the edge of complacency and indecision.

"*I do not know whether what I believe in is God or not.*" That is better. I am up off the couch, taking a step in the right direction, making a movement in the direction of passion, engaged in a more committed and passionate act, with a taste for faith. For here at least I recognize that life does not take a single step forward without faith, that if we are going to get anywhere, faith is first, last, and constant. I know that if I wait for all the results to come in, for definitive information to settle the matter, life will have long since left the station without me. I do believe, help thou (somebody) my unbelief. But I do not know in what I believe, or whether what I believe in is God or not, whether it should be addressed with the name of God. Perhaps I do not believe in God but in something else. Perhaps what I am responding to is the call of "life," its immanent energy and inner momentum. Perhaps I am embracing the auto-justifying exercise of life itself, for life is its own reward and it does not have to answer the question, "why desire life?". This is all true enough, but it is not enough truth, not passionate enough. It is still too much inclined to think that life is some sort of epistemic problem, a question of determining a "what" rather than of doing a "how," a question of identifying what we believe in or to what we are praying, rather than embracing the *how* of living full steam, with all the passion of love, the *how* of praying in spirit and in truth for I know not what.

"*What do I love when I love my God?*" Here I hit full stride, releasing all the passion of the impossible, all the energy of love. For who would be so hard of heart, so lacking in faith and love, as not to love God? You know that I love You, Augustine says, but the question is what do I love when I love You, my God? God is love. God is the name of love. God is the name of what we love, and the question is what do we love when we love God, love our God, love "You, my God?" The name of God is the most powerful, the most beautiful, the most indispensable name we have, the first among all names, at the sound of which every knee shall bend, the name we must revere and embrace, love and guard from its detractors. Those who are atheists about this God have no heart, no love – whoever does not love, does not love God – for they deny the love of God and the God of love. The name of God is the name of the ever open question. Unlike reductionists, who think that the name of God closes every question down, that it supplies a ready-made answer for every possible question, the name of God in my post-modern *Itinerarium* is the name of infinite questionability, of what is endlessly questionable, for no name can cause my head to spin more than the name of what I love and desire. But what do I love when I love my God? In loyalty to St. Augustine, whom I also love, I have retained the "what," but of course, if I dared to correct a Saint, which I would never do, if I were an obscure copyist in an Irish monastery in the tenth century working on the *Confessiones*, I would in all fear and trembling have furtively amended the *what* to a *how*. How do I love when I love my God? For love is a *how*, not a *what*.

And so is God. Over and above the creedal formulas and the councils, the theological treatises and the official prayer books of the official religions, which labor over the *what*, settling important questions like the *filioque* debate, God is a *how*, not a *what*. God is the passion of life, the passion of my life, the passion of my unknowing, my passion for the impossible. God is served in spirit and in truth, not in propositions. That we learn from a reliable source, a Jewish prophet with a taste for giving the Jews hell (holy hell) for their infidelities. You who turn justice to wormwood, who trample on the poor and push aside the needy, had best take care about calling for the day of the Lord, Amos warns them in his memorable fifth chapter, lest you get more than you bargained for. I hate your festivals and your solemn assemblies, and I will not accept your burnt offerings, Amos has the Lord God tell them. Take away your songs and your glorious liturgies, and the melodies of your harps – take away your "religions," Amos seems to say. "But let justice roll down like waters and righteousness like an ever-flowing stream" (Amos 5:24). The name of God is spoken in spirit and in truth, not by being sung in solemn assemblies, but in love, for whoever loves is born of God, and in "doing" justice, in making justice happen, which Amos describes as serving the poor and the needy, not stealing from them or letting them rot. Amos, I think, was among the first to propose the idea of "religion without religion," which means more justice and fewer burnt offerings and solemn assemblies. For Amos, the name of God is the name of justice, and justice is not a thought but a deed, and its truth is attained only in *doing* the truth, in making justice happen in truth. Justice is not had by talking the talk in solemn assemblies, but by walking the walk in the inner cities. The justice of God, the God of justice – that is a deed, a *how*.

Thus, at the end of these reflections *On Religion*, we learn, alas, that the distinction between theism and atheism, religion and unreligion, is beset by a certain confusion and subject to the holy undecidability that I have been analyzing. For religion is the love of God, which is living and life-transforming when justice rolls down like waters, which is also denied when justice is denied. "Those who say 'I love God' and hate their brothers or sisters, are liars" (I John 4:2). Justice takes place inside and outside the historical religions, inside, with the Dietrich Bonhoeffers and Mother Teresas and countless nameless saints who lead lives of quiet and obscure heroism serving the least among us while the rest of us are leading lives of ease. And outside, for there is no safely secular sphere where we can be so sure that no religious fires burn. Religion – with or without religion – wherever there are men and women who love and serve justice, who love and serve God.

Where are you, my God?

If God is a deed, not a thought, then that puts in perspective and gives us a way of sorting through the profusion of nonsense that is readily available in any Barnes and Noble store or on the Amazon.com website in which the love of God gets confused with New Age poppycock like the Celestine prophecy, celestial visitations by angels, channelings, sightings of Elvis, UFOs, or God knows what! The love of God has nothing to do with the idle curiosities – what Augustine (following I John 2:16) called the curiosities of the eyes (*curiositas occulorum*) – of well-heeled, middle-aged baby boomers looking for amusement. It has to do with the transformability of our lives, with the possibility of a transforming future, and with serving the poorest and most defenseless people in our society, with welcoming the strangers who make their way across our well-defended borders, the homeless and the abandoned, the ill and the aging. Lord, when did we see you hungry and give you to eat (Matt. 25:37)?

God is not playing a great guessing game with us in which we all sit around and take a stab at who or what is going on behind a great cosmic curtain that has been drawn down before us. The withdrawal of God is not the occasion of amusement for the curious or of puzzlement for the metaphysicians. The withdrawal of God from our view is always a matter of justice, of God's deflecting our approach from God to the neighbor, as the Jewish philosopher Emmanuel Levinas says, a structural declining to be made visible or palpable in order to produce justice for the neighbor and the stranger. The *deflection* of God is the *translation* of God into a deed: Lord, when did we see You thirsty and give You to drink? It requires *doing* things, not philosophizing or theologizing them half to death. Philosophy and theology have their place, and I am myself very fond of (even addicted to) both of them, but they can prove to be a distraction, a *curiositas*. People who are doing justice but have no theology or philosophy, no list of approved creedal pronouncements, or even a name of God at their disposal, are far closer to what the Rhineland mystic Meister Eckhart liked to call the "divine God." As opposed to the human one, the God of the raft, the one we enjoy speculating about, or making guesses about, or dismissing as an illusion, as if God were an even higher-flying and still more unidentifiable UFO. Unless you *are* this poverty about which I am preaching, Eckhart said in one of his sermons, do not waste your time trying to understand me.

Religion in the sense of the love of God cannot contain what it contains. We have defined religion in terms of the love of God, but the love of God cannot be defined – or contained – by religion. The love of God is too important to leave to the religions or the theologians.

When it comes to loving God, who is in and who is out?

We get a clue from a very famous parable in the New Testament, which tells a story about a wedding party madder than any party ever imagined by Lewis Carroll (Matt. 22:1–14). When none of the guests who have been invited show up for the wedding feast, the host sends his servants out into the streets to bring in the strangers and casual passers-by who just happen to be in the neighborhood, who are not dressed for the occasion, and who do not even know the bride and groom. Can you imagine a more unimaginable and unbelievable wedding reception than that? But that, we are told, is how the "Kingdom of God" works. The Christians composed this story as a way of putting it to the Jews, who rejected Jesus (a tactic not unknown to "John," the author of the gospel and epistles of love, I might add), but of course, the story has a kick to it and boomerangs equally on Christian exclusivism. In the Kingdom, the insiders are out, have missed out, while the outsiders are in! The Kingdom of God, the place where God's love rules, does not turn on formal invitation lists and formal memberships, but includes anyone who does justice in spirit and in truth. Anyone who loves is born of God. The Kingdom of God is a *how*, not a *what*.

What do I love when I love my God? Not the burnt offerings and solemn assemblies, but justice. Is justice then another name for God? Or is God another name for justice? We have insisted all along upon the undecidability of this sort of question, to which we should add now an insistence upon its pointlessness. If I serve the neighbor in the name of God, or if I serve the neighbor in the name of justice, what difference does it make? If the name of God is a *how*, not a *what*, then the name of God is *effective* even when it is not used. Perhaps it is *more* effective, more of a "force," as George Lucas might say, if it is not even known, because then the name of

God, and the love of God, can stay clear of all the complications of human "religion."

The *meaning* of God is *enacted*, or else it is refused and we devote our time instead to building up our stock portfolios. It is enacted equally but differently in Mahatma Gandhi, who waged non-violent battle with evil, in the life and death of Jesus, who was executed because of the subversiveness of his message that the One he dared called Abba has forgiven us, even as it is enacted in the reverence of Chief Joseph for the majesty of the natural world, who expressed astonishment at the perversity of the white man's idea that the earth belongs to human beings instead of recognizing that we belong to the earth. The love of God is enacted whenever our human, all too human drives are contradicted and thrown into reverse and we are drawn out of ourselves by something larger or other than ourselves, when our powers and potencies come unhinged and we are left hanging by a prayer for the impossible.

The *meaning* of God is enacted in an openness to a future that I can neither master nor see coming, in an exposure to possibilities that are impossible for me, which surpass my powers, which overpower me, which drive me to the limits of the possible, which draw me out to God, *à Dieu*. With whom nothing is impossible.

What do I love when I love my God? To a Buddhist, or to a native American, or to a contemporary eco-feminist, the cosmos is not a blind and stupid rage, as Nietzsche thought, but a friend, our element and matrix, the beginning and the end, the gentle rocking of a great cosmic womb, a friendly flux from which we take our origin and to which we return, like the steady beat of ten thousand waves in the sea. Then the love of God means to learn how to dance or swim, to learn how to join in the cosmic play, to move with its rhythms, and to understand that we are each of us of no special import other than to play our part in the cosmic ballet. In Judaism and Christianity, on the other hand, the name of God is the name of the One who has counted every tear and has numbered every hair on our heads. That makes each individual precious, a lost sheep or a lost coin, a lost son or a lost daughter, and the name of God is the name of the good shepherd who sets out in search of the single sheep who is lost while the other ninety-nine are safe, or of the parent ("father") who forgives the lost child ("prodigal son") and throws a party to celebrate the child's return even though the child has squandered everything. That does not mean that this Lord of history is not the same Lord of the elements who rides on the wings of the wind and waters the cedars of Lebanon in the majestic 104th Psalm.

The meaning of God is enacted in these multiple movements of love, but these movements are simply too multiple, too polyvalent, too irreducible, too uncontainable to identify, define, or determine. By asking Augustine's question, "what do I love when I love my God?", we concede that the love of God is radically, or ineradicably, translatable, that we cannot contain the process of substitution or translation that it sets in motion. But this translation is not a semantic process but an existential or pragmatic one. It is not a matter of finding a dictionary equivalent for the love of God but of doing it, of giving testimony to it, of seeing that its effect is to translate us into action, to move and bestir us. Love is not a meaning to define but something to do, something to make. When we pondered the translatability or substitutability of these two terms, "God" and "love," and we asked which is a translation of which, we were looking in the wrong place for a translation. In the translatability of the love of God it is we who are to be translated, transformed, and carried over into action, carried off by the movements of love, carried away by the transcendence that this name names and commands. The translation of the love of God is transcendence; it is the movement that it names, the deed that it demands, for the love of God is something to *do*. The love of God is not explained or explicated in a proposition but testified to, enacted, performed.

"God" – that is not only a name but an injunction, an invitation, a solicitation, to commend, to let all things be commended, to God.

To God.

ADIEU

What, then, do I love when I love my God?
God be with you.
Thank you, Jesus, thank you!
Oui, oui!
Adieu (à Dieu).

Bibliographical Note and Acknowledgments

The scriptural citations are from *The Holy Bible: The New Revised Standard Version* (Nashville: Thomas Nelson, 1989). Augustine's *Confessions* is available in numerous translations, but I like the translation by Frank Sheed (Indianapolis: Hackett, 1970), a consultation of which will reveal the heavy use I have been making of Book X in particular. Garry Wills, *Saint Augustine* (New York: Viking Penguin, 1999) is as good a general introduction to St. Augustine as one would ever want. I have analyzed the complexities of the work of Jacques Derrida, which is always in the background of this book, in a more detailed way in my *The Prayers and Tears of Jacques Derrida: Religion Without Religion* (Bloomington: Indiana University Press, 1997); modesty prevents me from recommending *Deconstruction in a Nutshell: A Conversation with Jacques Derrida* (New York: Fordham University Press, 1997) as a lucid and lively introduction to Derrida. I have also cited Terry Brooks, *Star Wars, Episode I: The Phantom Menace* (New York: Ballantine, 1999); *Kierkegaard's Writings*, VI, "Fear and Trembling" and "Repetition," trans. Howard and Edna Hong (Princeton: Princeton University Press, 1983).

I am grateful to general editors Richard Kearney and Simon Critchley, and my Routledge editor Tony Bruce for inviting me to write this book and for their very helpful advice, and to my friend Dr. Keith Putt, without whose sage counsel this book would be even more heterodox than it has turned out to be.

Index